SpringerBriefs in Well-Being and Quality of Life Research

More information about this series at http://www.springer.com/series/10150

William P. O'Hare

Data-Based Child Advocacy

Using Statistical Indicators to Improve
the Lives of Children

 Springer

William P. O'Hare
The Annie E. Casey Foundation
Baltimore, MD
USA

ISSN 2211-7644   ISSN 2211-7652   (electronic)
ISBN 978-3-319-07829-8   ISBN 978-3-319-07830-4   (eBook)
DOI 10.1007/978-3-319-07830-4

Library of Congress Control Number: 2014944722

Springer Cham Heidelberg New York Dordrecht London

Printed on acid-free paper

Springer is part of Springer Science+Business Media (www.springer.com)

Introduction

Within the broad field of child advocacy a subset of advocates has emerged in recent years, who focus on using statistical data and scientific evidence to promote better lives for children. At the same time there are growing numbers of researchers and scholars who are using statistical data to provide a deeper understanding of children's lives. I call the intersection of data, statistics, and scientific evidence on the one hand and explicit efforts to improve the quality of life for children on the other hand, as "Data-Based Child Advocacy," which is the theme of this publication. As defined here, data-based child advocacy includes any activity where at least one central component is focused on improving the lives of children using statistical data. A more complete and detailed description of the term is offered in Chaps. 2 and 3.

There are four key points I try to make in this publication. First, growing numbers of individuals and organizations are combining data and advocacy to try and improve the lives of children. Second, there are many different activities combining data and advocacy that fit into the data-based child advocacy framework. Third, the development of data-based child advocacy is closely connected with several other recent trends. Fourth, combining communication expertise and data expertise is critical for successful data-based child advocacy.

I suspect much of what I present in this publication is not new to many readers. Most people who have an interest in this topic are already engaged in some way. What is new, I believe, is the way material is combined and conceptualized here as part of a larger framework called data-based child advocacy.

The conceptualization of *Data-Based Child Advocacy* offered in this publication provides a framework that will help identify which activities should be included as part of data-based child advocacy as well as the roles played by data experts and child advocates. Hopefully, such recognition will facilitate productive interaction between scholars, researchers, and child advocates and will ultimately improve the quality of life for children.

I think of advocacy and science as being ends of an activity continuum. At one end, some advocates pay no attention to data or scientific evidence. At the other end of the continuum, some scientists pay little attention to the social consequences of their research and make no attempt to get their findings before the public or policymaking audiences. However, there are many points along the continuum where scholarship and advocacy can be combined in ways that enhance both.

In this publication, I focus largely on statistical data or social indicators in discussing data-based child advocacy, though the term often reflects more than that. For example, the results of scientific evaluations of public policies and programs would be considered part of data-based child advocacy as would research results from scientific journals and textbooks. Efforts to collect and summarize scientific work and make such summaries available to broad audiences also fit into the data-based child advocacy conceptual framework. The focus on the use of descriptive social indicators of child well-being in this publication is partly due to space available, but it is also due to the fact that a discussion of statistical analysis and research publications in the context of data-based child advocacy is more complex. In addition, I believe that descriptive data provided by data books, report cards, and websites are at the heart of data-based child advocacy.

This publication includes information from around the world, but focuses on the United States more than other parts of the world. I focus on the United States partly because it is the landscape I know best. Also, I think data-based child advocacy is more advanced in the United States than in many other areas of the world. While a few points discussed here are particularly relevant to the United States' sociopolitical environment, I suspect most of the points discussed in this publication can be easily translated to other countries and other cultures.

The audience I hope to reach with this publication is diverse. There are many professionals, for example, in the areas of education and public health, who use data to reach nonscholarly audiences on a regular basis. I hope this publication helps them see how their work fits into a broader field of data-based child advocacy and I hope they may find information in this publication that will help them do their job more effectively.

One audience I hope to reach with this publication is those individuals who have been trained in quantitative social science methods, but have little or no experience or understanding of advocacy. In my experience, many scholars and researchers involved in mainstream academic research would like to see their work have a bigger impact on public discussions and/or public policy. Some of the lessons from this review of *Data-Based Child Advocacy* may be helpful in that regard.

Chapter 2 provides a detailed description of data-based child advocacy and a rationale for why data-based child advocacy is important and growing. In this chapter, the relatively unique situation of children with regard to advocacy is discussed.

Chapter 3 provides a list of six distinct uses of child indicators in advocacy-related activity with multiple examples given in each of the six areas. The level of detail provided in this chapter will help readers gain a deeper and richer understanding of *Data-Based Child Advocacy*. The material presented in Chap. 3 may also help some readers more clearly see how their work fits into the broader data-based child advocacy movement. Also, the material in this chapter underscores the extent to which data-based child advocacy is emerging in many different forms and contexts.

Chapter 4 provides some discussion of how the data-based child advocacy movement has developed. In this chapter, the connections between several other trends and the increase in data-based child advocacy are explored. Some of the reasons that data-based child advocacy is not more widely recognized are also covered in this chapter.

A section on communication, Chap. 5, is included in this volume because combining data and effective communication is critical for successful data-based child advocacy. Communication norms are perhaps the biggest differences between writing for scholarship and writing for public influence. In this chapter, I contrast styles and techniques that are different in public settings than they are in academic or scholarly settings.

It is often useful to know authors' background in order to understand their approach to a field and better understand potential biases. I am a demographer by training and I have spent nearly all of my work life in the nonprofit sector where I was writing for public audiences. I was also a contributing editor to the *American Demographics* magazine for about a dozen years. The material presented here is drawn partly from my 25-year involvement with the KIDS COUNT project in the U.S. (O'Hare 2013). While this experience is largely in the context of the United States, my thoughts have also been heavily shaped by my participation in the founding and development of the International Society for Child Indicators.

Reference

O'Hare, W. P. (2013). A case study of data-based child advocacy: The KIDS COUNT project. *Child Indicators Research, 6*(1), 33–52.

Contents

Chapter 1
What Is Data-Based Child Advocacy?

Data-based child advocacy is a term coined by The Annie E. Casey Foundation (Morgan 2001; The Annie E. Casey Foundation 2003; O'Hare 2007; International Society for Child Indicators 2009; Benjamin 2009) to refer to the use of data, statistics, and science to enhance discussion and debate about topics relevant to child well-being. Advocacy in this context is often not about supporting a certain piece of legislation or a specific policy; it is about using data to elevate public understanding and public awareness of problems and issues facing children. It is also about advocating for the public and political will to make changes needed to improve the lives of children.

A recent description of The Annie E. Casey's signature data-based initiative, KIDS COUNT (The Annie E. Casey Foundation 2010, p. 4) noted;

> Advocates, journalists, policymakers, practitioners, and all concerned citizens can find data for planning, preparing reports, crafting policies, or identifying and addressing needs in their community.

This describes the aspirations for how The Annie E. Casey Foundation hopes the data it provides will be used and fits neatly into the definition of data-based child advocacy offered in the first paragraph.

Over the past two decades there has been an enormous increase in the collection and use of social indicators related to children (Ben-Arieh and Frones 2009; Skocpol and Dickert 2001; O'Hare 2012; Brown et al. 2002; Brown and Botsko 1996; Brown 2008; Brown and Moore 2007; Stagner et al. 2008). Much of this literature fits into my definition of data-based child advocacy. The intent of much of this literature is captured in a quote from Ben-Arieh and Frones (2009, p. ix), "The measuring and monitoring of children's well-being is of growing importance to policymakers and those who strive to improve the lives of children everywhere."

© The Author(s) 2014
W.P. O'Hare, *Data-Based Child Advocacy*,
SpringerBriefs in Well-Being and Quality of Life Research,
DOI 10.1007/978-3-319-07830-4_1

One of the reasons there has been an increase in the kinds of activities that I define as data-based child advocacy, is recognition that what is sometimes described as "power politics" does not work well for children. Groups with significant political power can successfully interact and negotiate with elected officials directly while those without political power must rely on others to carry their message. Because they have little influence working directly with elected officials, child advocates often must use what Gormley (2012) calls an "outsider strategy." Outsider strategies include appeals to the general public through public policy research, press conferences, media outreach. Such efforts often include heavy use of statistical data.

The lack of political power among children has led individuals and organizations to search for other methods for persuading elected officials to support programs for children. One prominent review (Reid 2001, p. 106) of child advocacy groups concluded;

> Child advocacy groups use a wide range of activities to influence the decisions and practices of government, business, and society. Organizing public education, reporting findings to the public and to government officials and lobbying and testifying all build public awareness and support for policy issues.

Since most voters have a relatively positive view of children, advocates hope to elevate the political saliency of children's issues in a political context by using data to get media attention and sway voters.

I argue that in a democratic political context, solid data are more important for child advocates than for advocates representing most other groups because children are politically powerless. Children have a lot of political appeal but very little political clout. This perspective is consistent with Gormley and Cymrot (2006, p. 114) who reviewed child advocacy in America and concluded, "Child advocacy groups are different from most other groups in that they represent a constituency that is positively constructed but powerless." By that they mean that in a political context most advocates represent groups that can provide money (financial support for the next election) and/or votes if an elected official votes or makes a decision that benefits the group engaged in advocating. But children and child advocates have neither money nor votes to offer. This point is echoed by the United States child advocacy group, Every Child Matters (2013) which states, "Children don't vote and don't donate to campaigns, so it's up to all of us to speak up for them."

Ho (2014, p. A20) recently reported that the top ten lobbying firms in the United States had revenues of more that $226 million in 2013 but that is just the tip of the iceberg. According to analysis by the website Open Secrets.com, (http:// www.opensecrets.org/lobby/index.php), based on data it obtained from the Secretary of the Senate's Office of Public Records, $3.2 billion were spent on lobbyists in 2013. This does not include money spent by state-level lobbying groups. Child advocacy groups find it difficult to compete with groups that can spend millions of dollars to support their cause. In a report on child advocacy from few years ago (State Legislative Leaders Foundation 1995, p. 29), researchers found;

Leaders acknowledge that child and family groups lack the financial resources necessary to ensure legislative effectiveness. Constantly the comparison was made between advocates and well financed lobbyist.

Often the best things child advocates can offer is data and scientific evidence (and perhaps moral appeals).

This perspective is also supported by Reid (2001, p. 124) who concluded, "Decision makers are particularly interested in scientific information and advocates have learned to use it to promote their causes." Helping to make good data on children easily and readily available is a role scholars and data analysts can play to promote child well-being.

This is not to say that there aren't other groups who lack significant political power (for example the homeless population), but I would argue that none of these other groups are as large or as important as the child population. In the United States, children (people under age 18) represent a quarter of the population or nearly 75 million people (O'Hare 2013). Worldwide, there are 1.9 billion children and they make up 26 percent of the world's population (Population Reference Bureau 2013).

Moreover, no other group is as important to the future of the country or the world as children. The phrase "children are the future" may sound trite but it rings true with a large share of the public. Research shows early environments shape outcomes later in life and that investments made in children pay dividends later (National Research Council and Institute of Medicine 2000; Haywood and Gorman 2004; Karoly et al. 2005). As one publication put it (The Annie E. Casey Foundation 1990, p. 1), "Children make up one-quarter of this nation's population and all of its future."

At least in the United States, the relative political power of children compared to the elderly may explain why the proliferation of data-based reports on children has not been matched by similar reports on the elderly. Traditional power politics works for those advocating for the elderly because they have money and votes.

References

Benjamin, D. (2009). Framing in the field: A case study. *New directions for youth development* (Vol. 124, pp. 91–96). New York: Wiley Interscience.

Ben-Arieh, A., & Frones, I. (Eds.). (2009). *Indicators of children's well-being: Theory and practice in a multi-cultural perspective*. New York: Springer.

Brown, B. V., & Botsko, C. (1996). A guide to state and local-level indicators of child well-being available through the federal statistical system. Paper prepared for the Annie E. Casey Foundation, Baltimore MD.

Brown, B. V., Smith, B., & Harper, M. (2002). *International surveys of child and family well-being: An overview*. Washington DC: Child Trends Inc.

Brown, B. V., & Moore, K. A. (2007). *On overview of state-level data on child well-being available through the federal statistical system*. Washington DC: Child Trends.

Brown, B. V. (Ed.). (2008). *Key indicators of child and youth well-being: Completing the picture*. Mahwah, NJ: Lawrence Erlbaum.

Every Child Matters (2013, December). email Newsletter.
Gormley, W. T. (2012). *Voices for children: Rhetoric and public policy*. Washington, DC: Brookings Institution Press.
Gormely, W. T., & Cymrot, H. (2006). The strategic choices of child advocacy groups. *Nonprofit and Voluntary Sector Quarterly, 35*(1), 102–122.
Haywood, M. D., & Gorman, B. K. (2004). The long arm of childhood: The influence of early-life social conditions on men mortality. *Demography*, 41(1), 87–107.
Ho, C. (2014, January 24). Revenue down slightly at the biggest lobby shops. *The Washington Post* (p. A20).
International Society for Child Indicators (2009, May). *Recent conferences: NGOs Gather at Landmark Mexico Gathering, ISCI Newsletter.*
Karoly, L. A., Kilburn, M. R., & Cannon, J. S. (2005). *Early childhood interventions: Proven results future promise*. Santa Monica, CA: Rand Corporation.
Morgan, D. (2001). KIDS count self-assessment: bridging evaluation with strategic communication of data on children and families. *Evaluation exchange* (Vol 7(1)). Cambridge, MA: Winter, Harvard University.
National Research Council and Institute of Medicine (2000). *From neurons to neighborhoods*: *The science of early childhood development*. Washington, DC: National Academy Press.
O'Hare, W. P. (2007, January 7–9). Data-based child advocacy: Using demographic indicators to increase public awareness of child well-being in the United States. Paper presented at the Applied Demography Conference, San Antonio, TX.
O'Hare, W. P. (2012). Development of the child indicator movement in the United States. *Child Development Perspectives, 6*(1), 79–84.
O'Hare, W. P. (2013). What data from the 2010 census tell us about the changing child population of the United States. *Population Research and Policy Review, 32*(5), 767–789.
Population Reference Bureau (2013). *World population data sheet*. Washington, DC: Population Reference Bureau. http://www.prb.org/pdf13/2013-population-data-sheet_eng.pdf.
Reid, E. (2001). Building a policy voice for children through the nonprofit sector. In C. J., De Vita & R., Mosher-Williams (Eds.), *Who speaks for America's children? The role of child advocates and public policy* (pp. 105–133). Washington, DC: The Urban Institute Press.
Skocpol, T., & Dickert, J. (2001). Speaking for families and children in a changing civic america. In C. J. De Vita & R. Mosher-Williams (Eds.), *Who speaks for America's children? The role of child advocates and public policy* (pp. 137–164). Washington DC: The Urban Institute Press.
Stagner, M., Goerge, R. M., & Ballard, P. (2008). *Improved indicators of child well-being*. Chicago: Chapin Hall at the University of Chicago.
State Legislative Leaders Foundation (1995). *State legislative leaders: Keys to effective legislation for children and families, a report*. Centerville, MA: State Legislative Leaders Foundation.
The Annie E. Casey Foundation (1990). 1990 *KIDS COUNT Data Book*. Baltimore, MD: The Annie E. Casey Foundation.
The Annie E. Casey Foundation (2003). *Data-based advocacy*. Baltimore, MD: The Annie E. Casey Foundation.
The Annie E. Casey Foundation (2010). *The KIDS COUNT data book*. Baltimore, MD: The Annie E. Casey Foundation.

Chapter 2
Types of Advocacy Activity Using Child Indicators

Data-based child advocacy includes any activity where at least one central component is focused on improving the lives of children using statistical data or scientific evidence. Data-based child advocacy-related activities can be described and clustered many different ways but for purposes of this publication six different kinds of data-based child advocacy activities are identified and discussed;

1. Increasing public awareness about child well-being,
2. Making data on children more easily available,
3. Advocating for more and better data on children,
4. Monitoring child well-being,
5. Goal setting for child well-being, and
6. Evaluating programs and policies related to children.

There is considerable overlap among the six categories listed above and some activities actually belong in multiple categories. I have tried to be parsimonious, but some material may be referenced in more than one place.

2.1 Increasing Public Awareness About Child Well-Being

I would argue that using child indicators and data to raise public awareness about the well-being of children is the single biggest use of child indicators in an advocacy context. Growing numbers of indicator-based reports around the world are trying to educate the public and inform policymakers about the levels and trends in the well-being of children. Pollard and Lee (2003) found more than 1,600 articles they classified as being related to child well-being that were published between 1990 and 1999. Ben-Arieh (2006) found 199 "child reports" as of 2006. Interestingly, the vast majority of the reports found by Ben-Arieh were from governments, advocacy groups, and international organizations. Only 16 % of the 199 studies

© The Author(s) 2014
W.P. O'Hare, *Data-Based Child Advocacy*,
SpringerBriefs in Well-Being and Quality of Life Research,
DOI 10.1007/978-3-319-07830-4_2

were classified as academic. This reflects the strong advocacy orientation of such reports.

I think it is fair to say that the more reports there are on child well-being the more likely it is that they will increase public awareness about the problems facing children. In the words of Hood (2006, p. 249);

> Regular reports on the state of children are an essential tool in raising public awareness, achieving political support for improving children's living conditions and promoting and ensuring children's rights under the UN Convention on the Rights of the Child.

Below I review some of the key reports based on child indicators over the past few decades. I focus on recurring reports because I believe they have the most impact and visibility. It is important to recognize that this is not a complete listing of such reports, but just a sample of similar reports. The reports reviewed here are meant to provide readers with a better sense of the kinds of reports that I view as part of data-based child advocacy. This chapter also provides evidence that data-based child advocacy is widespread.

There are many ways to organize data-based reports on child well-being that have been issued in the past few decades. I discuss reports produced by international organizations first, then some country-specific reports, and finally the United States landscape. The United States is examined individually because it is the area that I know the best and I believe data-based child advocacy is relatively advanced there.

2.1.1 International Reports

On the international front, the United Nations has been a leader in data-based reports on children. The United Nations*State of the World's Children* (available at http://www.unicef.org/sowc/) annual report which began in 1979 has pioneered this type of data-rich publication. A recent report (United Nations 2014, p. i) captures the thrust of the report series;

> Thirty years have passed since *The State of the World's Children* began to publish tables of standardized global and national statistics aimed at providing a detailed picture of children's circumstances.
>
> Much has changed in the decades since the first indicators of child well-being were presented. But the basic idea has not: consistent, credible data about children's situations are critical to the improvement of their lives—and indispensable to realizing the rights of every child.

In terms of raising public awareness, another key development on the international front was the adoption of The United Nations Convention on the Rights of the Child (UNCRC) in 1990. The UNCRC fosters civil, political, economic, social and cultural rights of children (Doek 2014; Vuckovic et al. 2013). The UNCRC not only provides a framework for assessing the well-being of children, it fosters and promotes more measurement and reporting on child well-being around the globe

(United Nations 1989/1990). Article 44 of the Convention calls for regular reporting on child well-being by countries that have ratified the document.

Every country in the world except the United States, South Sudan, and Somalia has ratified the Convention on the Rights of the Child. The United States has signed the United Nations Convention on the Rights of the Child (during President Clinton's administration) but the United States has not ratified it. In the United States system in order to be ratified, the treaty would have to be passed by two-thirds of the Senate and signed by the President. Despite internal efforts to persuade the United States to ratify the UNCRC (Campaign for United States Ratification of the Convention on the Rights of the Child 2014), there is no indication that this is likely to happen soon and there is clearly some opposition to the United States ratifying the UNCRC (Kilbourne 1998).

The UNCRC has also stimulated production of child indicators. For example, Doek (2014, p. 212) concludes;

> With regard to measuring the impact of CRC's implementation, there is ongoing discussion on the development of indicators, with considerable attention focused on quantitative results, for example, statistics on infant mortality, malnutrition, and other health rates; education enrollment figures; and the number of children in institutions, foster care, and juvenile justice systems.

Another branch of the United Nations, UNICEF's Innocenti Research Centre in Florence, Italy, has produced a series of publications focused on various aspects of child well-being in developed countries. There are now nine publications in the Report Card series from the Innocenti Research Centre all published since 2000. Most of the report cards focus on measures of comprehensive child well-being among a set of developed countries. Collectively, these reports provide one of best sources of comparative statistical data about the well-being of children in more developed countries. The reports are available on the Centre's website at http://www.unicef-irc.org/publications/.

The UNICEF Multiple Indicator Cluster Surveys (MICS) initiative which started in the mid-1990s is now in the fourth round of surveys focused on measuring the well-being of children in less developed countries (available at http://www.unicef.org/statistics/index_24302.html). This initiative has generated an on-going series of publications based on measuring child well-being as well as a website where data are made available. According to the MICS website;

> Since the mid-1990s, the MICS has enabled many countries to produce statistically sound and internationally comparable estimates of a range of indicators in the areas of health, education, child protection and HIV/AIDS.

The adoption of the United Nations Millennium Development Goals has also fostered measurement and reporting on the well-being of children around the globe (United Nations 2000). While the United Nations Millennium Development Goals project is not about children per se, many of the Millennium Development Goals, such as reducing child mortality and achieving universal primary education, are directly related to the well-being of children, and other goals, such as improving maternal health and eradicating extreme poverty and hunger, are closely related to child well-being (United Nations 2000).

The work outlined above indicates that the United Nations has taken a leadership role in using data to increase public awareness of child well-being. I also want to emphasize the extent to which the work outlined above has been sustained over time because I strongly believe that repeated publications on a topic underscore an organizations commitment to that topic and repeated publications have more impact on policymakers and the public.

But the United Nations is not the only international organization engaged in such work. In recent years The Organisation for Economic Co-Operation and Development (OECD) has undertaken a large initiative to promote the use of statistical indicators for monitoring general social well-being and children have been a very visible part of this initiative. In addition to comprehensive reports on child well-being (OECD 2009), OECD has established a website where information can be shared and views among scholars can be exchanged (http://www. wikiprogress.org/index.php/Child_well-being). The thrust of the OECD initiative is captured in the Istanbul Declaration signed by several international organizations. In part the Istanbul Declaration (available at http://www.Organization for Economic Cooperation and Development.org/site/worldforum06/) says;

> We urge statistical offices, public and private organizations, and academic experts to work alongside representatives of their communities to produce high-quality, fact-based information that can be used by all of society to form a shared view of societal well-being and its evolution over time.

OECD has held a series of international meetings on statistics, knowledge and power under their "Measuring Progress of Societies" initiative and the topic of child well-being has been reflected in such meetings (Ben-Arieh and Gross-Manos 2009).

A variety of international Non-Governmental Organizations (NGOs) have contributed to the collective effort to increase awareness of child well-being as well. For example, over the past decade The Save the Children UK organization has produced a series for reports that use child well-being indicators to raise awareness of specific programs and their yearly publication of the Child Development Index has become a staple publication (Save the Children UK 2012).

2.1.2 Country Reports

Over the past two decades several countries have begun producing regularly updated reports on the well-being of children based on child indicators. Eleven such reports are identified in Table 2.1. I want to emphasize the reports listed in Table 2.1 and the reports covered here are only a sample of such reports. With the exception of the report on Mexico, the only reports covered here are those in English, and even within those written in English, I am sure I have not identified

Table 2.1 Data-based reports on children from selected countries

Australian Institute of Health and Welfare, Making Progress: The health, development and wellbeing of Australia's children and young people http://www.aihw.gov.au/publicaitons/index. cfm/title/10653
Canadian Council for Social Development Report: The progress of Canada's children http:// www.ccsd.ca/pubs/2002/pcc02/index.htm
Israel National Council for the child report, the state of the child in Israel: A statistical abstract http://www.children/org.il/pro_articles-list-eng.asp?ProjectID=35
South African Child Gauge Report: http://www.ci.org.za/depts/ci/pubs/pdf/general/gauge2013/ SouthAfricanChildGauge2013.pdf
Kinder Intel Report (Netherlands) www.kinderrenintel.nl
State of the Nation's Children;Office of the Minister of Children and Youth Affairs Report (Ireland) www.omc.gov.ie
South African Child Gauge Report: http://www.ci.org.za/depts/ci/pubs/pdf/general/gauge2013/ SouthAfricanChildGauge2013.pdf
Red por los Derechos de la Infancia en Mexico (Children's Rights Network in Mexico): México KIDS COUNT Report/La Infancia Cuenta: www.infanciacuenta.org
United States Reports
Children's Defense Fund http://www.childrensdefense.org/site/Pperver?pagename=policyareas_ stateamericaschildren_2008
Federal Interagency Forum on Child and Families Statistics http://www.childstats.gov
Foundation for Child Development's Child Well-Being Index http://www.soc.duke.edu/~cwi/
The Annie E. Casey Foundation http://www.kidscount.org
KIDS COUNT www.kidscount.org

Over the past decade several countries have began producing regular reports on the well-being of children. Some reports are produced by government agencies while others are produced by Non-Governmental Organizations within the country

them all. Nonetheless, I think the reports covered here are representative of the broader set of reports and will give readers a flavor of this kind of activity.

The reports in Table 2.1 are produced by a mix of government agencies and non-profits or Non-Government Organizations (NGOs), often with the involvement of university scholars. They are similar in the fact that they all rely heavily on statistical indicators to provide a broad portrait of child well-being and they have all been published on a fairly regular basis over the past ten years or more. They often serve two advocacy-related purposes: raising public awareness and making data more easily available.

Consistent with the primary thrust of data-based child advocacy, it is the intention of most, if not all, of these country reports to stimulate some type of action to improve the lives of children. A quote from the Israel report captures a common sentiment;

> This report is more than just a passive portrayal or silent image of the world of children in Israel. It should serve as a vital tool in safeguarding of the rights of children in Israel and as a basis for taking action to improve their welfare. (Israel National Council for the Child Report 2007, p. iii).

In discussing the report from Ireland one prominent official stated;

The *State of the Nation's Children: Ireland 2008* is an important resource for all those who
seek to understand the experience of childhood in Ireland. As such, it will help us in our
task of making Ireland a better place for children. (Andrews 2008, p. iii).

It is also notable that the production of country reports on the well-being of
children is not just happening in the most developed countries of the world. For
example, in South Africa, the Children's Institute at the University of Cape Town
has produced a publication called *South African Children's Gauge* , regularly since
2005 (Children's Institute 2013). According to one source (Price 2009, p. 6);

The South African Children's Gauge, now in its fourth year of publication, has gained a
reputation as in invaluable resource that monitors the country's progress in realizing
children's constitutional rights.

In Mexico the non-profit group Red por Los Derechos de la Infancia in Mexico
(Children Rights Network) has produced a publication called *La Infancia Cuenta
en Mexico* (Kids Count in Mexico) for the past several years, which provides
measures of child well-being for the states of Mexico. A rough translation of one
passage in the 2010 Book (Red Por Los Derechos de la Infancia in Mexico 2010,
p. 5) says, "We hope this edition of the publication will facilitate access to the
information necessary for defense and promotion of the rights of children in our
country."

The data-based child advocacy movement is slowly developing in Latin
America, but it may not be as apparent there as other parts of the world because it
is largely reflected in non-English language publications. I asked two colleagues
who are familiar with data-based child advocacy in Latin America to provide a
short summary of some of the work there (See Appendix 1).

2.1.3 United States

There was a volume on child well-being published by the U.S. Department of
Health and Human Services (1980), almost simultaneously with the United
Nations State of the Worlds Child Report, but it did not get much public attention
and was not repeated. The development of the child indicator movement in the
United States is reflected in a series of yearly ongoing comprehensive reports on
child well-being that have emerged over the past 30 years (O'Hare 2012a). The
four ongoing reports covered here are;

- *State of America's Children*, produced yearly since 1981 by Children's Defense
  Fund,
- *KIDS COUNT Data Book*, produced yearly since 1990 by The Annie E. Casey
  Foundation,
- *America's Children; Key Indicators of Well-Being*, produced yearly since 1997
  by United States Federal Interagency Forum on Child and Family Statistics,

- *Child Well-Being Index* produced yearly since 2004 by the Foundation for Child Development.

Each of these initiatives is discussed below.

The Children's Defense Fund (CDF) started producing their annual *State of Americas Children* report around 1981. The most recent version of this annual report is available at http://www.childrensdefense.org/child-research-data-publications/data/2014-soac.pdf.

The *State of America's Children Report* is a comprehensive report on the well-being of children in the United States based on the latest data. Like many earlier reports, the 2014 report provides plentiful child indicators for each state and contains a media-friendly section showing all the negative events that happen in a typical day to American children, with a special emphasis on racial disparities. The *State of America's Children* report does not combine indicators into an overall index of child well-being and does not rank states on individual indicators or overall child well-being.

The *KIDS COUNT Data Book* produced by The Annie E. Casey Foundation has been published each year since 1990 and has gained a lot of visibility among journalists, advocates, and policymakers, in part, because the Foundation has used its resources to heavily promote and disseminate the publication. Many key audiences such as state legislators and Congressional staff report that they regularly use the data in the KIDS COUNT report and say that the KIDS COUNT report has had an impact on public policy in America (National Conference of State Legislators 2004, The Annie E. Casey Foundation 2005a, b, c, 2007; O'Hare 2008). More information about the KIDS COUNT program and the most recent version of the annual report are available at www.kidscount.org.

The 2011 edition of the *KIDS COUNT Data Book* (The Annie E. Casey Foundation 2011, P. 37) reiterates the primary purpose of KIDS COUNT report, "It is our hope that the *KIDS COUNT Data Book* and the accompanying KIDS COUNT Data Center will help raise the visibility of children's issues on the national agenda and serve as a tool for advocates, policymakers and others to make better decisions." This quote speaks to the Foundations desire to see the KIDS COUNT data used to improve child well-being.

The effectiveness of the KIDS COUNT initiative is due in part to the fact that the Casey Foundation has funded a KIDS COUNT program in every state. Since 1991 these state level organizations have produced hundreds of data-driven reports on child well-being in their state. (For a list of state KIDS COUNT organizations see http://www.aecf.org/MajorInitiatives/KIDSCOUNT/KIDSCOUNTStateNetwork.aspx).

In 1994, staff in several United States federal government statistical agencies informally initiated the Federal Interagency Forum on Child and Family Statistics. The "Forum," which now has 22 agency members, was formally established through Executive Order No. 13045, issued by President Clinton in April 1997. The Forum's mission (Wallman 2011, p. iii) is "to develop priorities for collecting enhanced data on children and youth, improve communication of information on the status of children to the policy community and the general public, and produce a more complete data on children at the Federal, state, and local levels."

The Forum is involved in many activities, but the most visible is their report called *America's Children: Key Indicators of Well-Being*, which has been published annually since 1997. The most recent edition as well as past editions of this annual report are available on line at http://childstats.gov. The *America's Children Report* differs from the KIDS COUNT and CDF reports because it is focused on national-level data rather than state-level data (O'Hare et al. 2013a).

According to the press release accompanying the 2011 report, (http://www.childstats.gov/americaschildren/press_release.asp);

> The report provides statistical information on children and families in a non-technical, easy-to-use format to stimulate discussion among data providers, policymakers, and members of the public.

I think this speaks to the Forum's interest in getting this information into the hands of a broad audience.

In addition to the government-wide report on children published each year by the Interagency Forum, many United States statistical agencies, such as the Census Bureau, the National Center on Education Statistics and the National Center on Health Statistics, also produce child indicator reports on a regular basis.

In short, many parts of the United States government provide data on the well-being of children. Again, this is just a sample of data on children available from United States government statistical agencies. Several authors (Brown 2008; Brown and Botsko 1996) provide a more complete accounting of child data from federal statistical agencies.

The Child Well-Being Index (CWI) created by the Foundation for Child Development was first reported in a peer-reviewed journal article in 2001 (Land et al. 2001). Starting in 2004, the CWI report has been released each year using the same 28 indicators clustered into seven domains of well-being (Foundation for Child Development 2013). The most recent edition of this annual report as well as past editions are available at http://fcd-us.org/our-work/child-well-being-index-cwi. The CWI report differs from the Forum's *America's Children* report largely because it has more historical data (back to 1976), it provides an annual index of well-being highlighting changes over time in overall child well-being, and the theoretical basis for indicator selection is more explicit.

In addition to the yearly CWI report, CWI methodology and data sources have been used to examine differences in child well-being, by gender, race, age, and international differences (among major English-speaking countries). The regular yearly CWI report only focuses on national level data but the CWI framework has also been used to look at variations across states (Lamb and O'Hare 2013; O'Hare et al. 2013b). The development of the index has also been the springboard for scholarly examination of issues related to measuring child well-being. For example, see the assembly of papers generated by a conference at the Brookings Institute in 2006 (available at http://www.brookings.edu/events/2006/0510welfare.aspx).

Nearly every year the CWI report has been covered by at least one large national newspaper in the United States such as *The New York Times*, *The Wall Street Journal*, *The Washington Post* or *USA Today* that reach millions of potential readers. The good media coverage is linked to thoughtful marketing and a strategic release strategy. The report is almost always released in Washington DC., (it has often been released at a special event held at the United States Capitol) and often involves one or more prominent elected official.

I want to mention two other closely-related report series that are slightly different than the four series described above. First Focus (2013) has been issuing a report called *Children's Budget* each year since 2007 that shows how the interests of children are reflected in the United States Federal budget. This report series is the first sustained look at how the Federal government supports (or doesn't support) children with dollars. And a companion report issued each year since 2007 called *Kids' Share* (Isaacs et al. 2013) shows similar data from a historical and projections perspective. While these two reports do not use measures that are typically thought of as child well-being indicators, they are data-rich and provide useful information about children in a public policy context.

The annual reports series discussed above have all emerged in the past 30 years and reflect the growing interest in data-based reports on child well-being. Collectively these annual reports on the well-being of children in the United States have raised public awareness about the well-being of children in a mutually re-enforcing way.

Several non-governmental organizations have also contributed to the child indicator movement in the United States. For example, the Washington-based nonprofit research organization Child Trends has developed an online data bank with information on numerous measures of child well-being (available at http://www.childtrends.org/databank/). Child Trends also produces a regular newsletter called *The Child Indicator* as a way to help keep the child indicator community informed about developments. Each issue of *The Child Indicator* goes out to about 13,000 potential readers. Child Trends also issues many data-driven publications on child well-being each year.

Chapin Hall at the University of Chicago is the home of the Child Monitoring Project, which provides information from early efforts to measure and monitor child well-being. The Multi-National Project for Monitoring and Measuring Children's Well-Being is an ongoing, multi-phase effort to improve our ability to measure and monitor the status of children around the globe. The National Center for Children in Poverty has also produced a number of data-driven reports on child well-being over the past 20 years. More information is available on their website at http://nccp.org/.

Data-based reports on children can help increase policymakers and the public understanding of children's issues, but regular publications on the well-being of children are also important because they signal that this is an important topic. If there were no prominent regular reports on the well-being of children, there may be an unconscious understanding that the well-being of children is not an important topic on the public agenda. Moreover, using data to generate public interest in improving the lives of children can put political pressure on policymakers to enact programs to enhance child well-being.

In summary, there are growing numbers of individuals and groups in a variety of settings working to increase public awareness about the well-being of children by publishing data-based reports. The sample of reports and efforts outlined here are all relatively new (within past few decades) and clearly such efforts are increasing. I believe the efforts outlined above are a fundamental part of the data-based child advocacy movement.

2.2 Making Data on Child Well-Being Easily Available

In some ways making data easily available overlaps with raising public awareness, but I believe there is a distinct set of efforts focused on getting data into the hands of decision makers and the broader public that is part of data-based child advocacy.

Many of the publications reviewed in Sect. 2.1 and the websites in Tables 2.1 and 2.2, are examples of how data on child well-being are being made widely available. Thirty years ago none of these publications or website existed. Despite the rapid increase in such activity over the past two decades, there are still many gaps in the data available on child well-being.

There are at least two key issues involved with making data more readily and easily available. One issue is related to increasing the amount and quality of data on children made available by government agencies and a second issue is making such data available in a form that is more usable for non-scholarly audiences. Scholars and researchers have a special role to play in both of these issues.

Data-based child advocates can play an important role by encouraging government statistical agencies and other groups involved in gathering data on children to make such data available to the public. They can also provide feedback to government agencies in terms of the kinds and amount of data they make available. Often times statisticians or data experts working in government agencies don't have a clear idea of how the data they release is perceived or used by the public.

If government agencies are unable or unwilling to make data available, data-based child advocates can play an important role by locating data in government files and making it more easily available through printed reports and/or websites. This activity is reflected in many publications discussed in the previous section. By gathering data from several different sources and putting it together in a data book or website, data-based child advocates can foster better and more holistic understanding of children and youth.

Researchers and data analysts can play an important role because they often have an understanding of the kinds of data collected by different statistical agencies. If data on children are buried in a government agency files, they are effectively unavailable to the non-scholars. Data-based child advocacy groups can

Table 2.2 Selected websites with child well-being Indicators

(1) The Annie E. Casey KIDS COUNT Project—www.kidscount.org
(2) The United States Federal Forum on Child and Family Statistics—www.childstats.gov
(3) Foundation for Child Development Child Well-Being Index—http://www.fcd-us.org/resources/2010-child-well-being-index-cwi
(4) Child Trends Data Bank-http://www.childtrendsdatabank.org/
(5) Chapin Hall/University of Chicago Child Monitoring Project http://multinational-indicators.chapinhall.org/
(6) International Data Base at United States Census Bureau http://www.census.gov/ipc/www/idb/
(7) International Society for Child Indicators (ISCI) http://www.childindicators.org/
(8) UNICEF Innocenti Research Centre http://www.unicef-irc.org/
(9) UNICEF Innocenti Research Centre Data Base
http://www.unicef-irc.org/databases/
(10) UNICEF Monitoring Statistics http://www.unicef.org/statistics/index.html
(11) UnitedNations Convention on the Rights of the Child http://www.unhchr.ch/html/menu3/b/k2crc.htm
(12) Chapin Hall/University of Chicago Child Monitoring Project http://multinational-indicators.chapinhall.org/
(13) Child Trends Data Bank- http://www.childtrendsdatabank.org/
(14) International Society for Child Indicators (ISCI) http://www.childindicators.org/
(15) Foundation for Child Development Child Well-Being Index—http://www.fcd-us.org/resources/2010-child-well-being-index-cwi
(16) The Annie E. Casey KIDS COUNT Project—www.kidscount.org
(17) The United States Federal Forum on Child and Family Statistics—www.childstats.org
(18) UNICEF Innocenti Research Centre http://unicerf-irc.org
(19) UNICEF Innocenti Research Centre Data Base http://www.unicef-irc.org/databases/
(20) UNICEF Monitoring Statistics http://www.unicef.org/statistics/index.html
(21) United Nations Convention on the Rights of the Child http://www.unhchr.ch/html/menu3/b/k2crc.htm

play an important role by making sure such information is more accessible to broad audiences.

In the United States federal government, many statistical agencies seem like an unsolvable maze for people who are unfamiliar with them. Yet the success of many data-based child advocacy initiatives rests partly on finding such data and making statistical indicators easily available to the public. Child indicator experts typically know how to find data on the well-being of children in government reports and/or websites, while many advocates and policymakers do not. Providing a bridge between government statistical agencies and public or non-scholarly audiences is an important role data-based child advocates can play.

It also important to distinguish between nominal availability of data and availability of data in a form that is usable by people without data or statistical skills or experience. There are at least two components to this issue. Sometimes, government agencies release data that is too complicated for a non-scholarly audience. Data-based child advocates can play an important role in translating complicated or unclear measures into something the lay public understands.

Another issue relates to how data is made available. For example computer-readable files are sometimes made available by government agencies. Such files can be very powerful and helpful for groups who have the human resources to download and analyze them using statistical software. Analyzing computer files to make data available to those without the resources to access computerized data is an important activity for researchers and data analysis.

But for many group, particularly under-funded child advocacy organizations, and the public at large, data on those files are effectively out of reach because they do not have the resources to purchase and process the data files.

Here is one example of how a non-profit organization helped make data available. During the 1990s, there were no regularly published comparable state figures on high school dropout rates in the United States. The federal government did not produce a set of comparable numbers and the figures produced by states were not comparable. The Annie E. Casey Foundation used a rolling 5-year average from the Census Bureau's Current Population Survey (CPS) to produce state-level indicators for high school dropout rates (O'Hare and Pollard 1998). These data could only be generated by purchasing the CPS micro-data files from the Census Bureau, processing them using statistical software and combining five consecutive years together to produce a large enough sample size for reliable state estimates. Most child advocacy organizations do not have the capacity to do this.

Another potential problem involves lack of statistical or mathematic skills; for example skills needed to convert counts into meaningful percentages or rates which are often needed to make comparisons among geographic units or socio-demographic groups. If a government agency provides the number of children in poverty and the total number of children, it is easy for a trained analyst to calculate a poverty rate. Many tables provided by the United States Census Bureau's American Factfinder software only provide such counts.

The provision of raw data or counts rather than percentages can be helpful because they allow users to combine data in ways that are more useful for them, but it can be problematic for people not accustomed to using data. For people who are drawn to data and statistics, it is difficult to imagine there are people unable to make such a calculation, but for those are not mathematically or statistically inclined, such a calculation may be beyond their ability. A recent report by the United States Department of Education (2013) found U.S. adults ranked 21st out of 23 countries in terms of numeracy. The survey found roughly 30 % of adults in the United States had relatively low numeracy skill levels compared to about 19 % for all countries combined. And it is important to recognize that some of these people are in important decision-making positions. Consequently, providing data in easy-to-understand forms is important.

Given the problems identified above, scholars, researchers, and scientists can play an important role in data-based child advocacy by helping to make data more readily available in a form that is useful to a broad public. Scholars, researchers, and scientists often know where data are located within the government bureau-cracy, they can assess the quality of the data, they know which indicators are typically more powerful, they have the computer skills needed to access the data, and they often have some presentation skills such as map making or chart making.

Methods for making information available are rapidly changing. The use of the internet and websites are increasing rapidly. Some of the implications of the growing influence of the internet are discussed in Chap. 5. However, Table 2.2 provides URLs for a sample of websites that now provide statistical data on children.

The Child Trends Data Bank is one such source of child indicators in the United States. The Data Bank is described as "…a one-stop source for the latest national trends and research on over 100 key indicators of child and youth well-being." (Child Trends 2011). This is just one more example of new sources of statistical indicators of child well-being that are being made available.

The KIDS COUNT initiative has moved from being solely focused on printed publications when it started in 1990, to having a website that provides more than 100 measures of child well-being for all states. The KIDS COUNT website is designed for users without a lot of statistical or computer skills so it is user-friendly and intuitive. It is also powerful because it allows users to create their own tabulations, charts and maps. The switch from printed form to a web-based form of dissemination allowed the KIDS COUNT initiative to not only make more data available, it allowed the staff to make data available more quickly.

The Organisation for Economic Co-Operation and Development has developed a website (WIKICHILD) that provides data on children and families from many countries, and the Multiple-Indicators Cluster Surveys also have a portal for obtaining data online.

Chapin Hall at The University of Chicago is the home of the Child Monitoring Project which provides information from early efforts to measure and monitor child well-being (more information about the Chapin Hall Child Monitoring Project is available online at http://multinational-indicators.chapinhall.org/).

The United States National Survey of Children's Health (NSCH) which has been fielded in 2003, 2007 and 2011, provides state level indicators of child well-being on a broad spectrum of topics related to child well-being. A few summary reports have been issued based on the data but one of the most innovative aspects is the NSCH website (http://www.childhealthdata.org/learn/NSCH) which allows users to produce customized tabulations from their survey data.

In summary, many sources of data on the well-being of children have emerged over the past few decades that help make statistical information more easily available to both scholars and non-scholarly audiences. Making child well-being data readily available provides an important use of indicators in an advocacy context and another link between scholars and those advocating for children. The dramatic increase in this kind of activity over the past few decades can be seen as another reflection of the growth of data-based child advocacy movement.

2.3 Advocating for More and Better Data on Children

The interests of child advocates and child researchers clearly overlap in advocating for data needed to better measure and monitor child well-being. Data availability is critical for assessing many government functions such as policy development and program administration. Many of the reports referenced in Sect. 2.1 would not have been possible unless someone had successfully advocated for the production and release of data on children.

The vast majority of data used in data-based child advocacy is collected by government agencies, either directly or by funding other organizations such as universities and NGOs. So influencing such agencies is an important aspect of data-based child advocacy.

The connection between child indicator experts and government agencies has evolved differently in different countries. In some countries, researchers already work very closely with government agencies to develop data on children. In other countries, researchers sometimes play more of an outside advocacy role (The Annie E. Casey Foundation 2009a, Stagner et al. 2008).

This is a bit of an oversimplification, but there are three main data-related tasks undertaken by government statistical agencies. First, government agencies determine what data to collect. Second, of the data collected by government agencies, a decision must be made about what to tabulate and/or analyze. And third, government agencies determine what data to make available to researchers and the public. There are potential advocacy activities associated with each of these steps.

Scholars can lend their expertise and weight to efforts to make sure government data collection activities use the best data collection methodologies, include the most accurate and reliable measures of child well-being, and make sure the data are made easily available in a timely fashion. Child indicators scholars generally have a lot of expertise and credibility on all of these issues.

Data-advocacy is needed because data production is generally a low priority within policy-making circles and is often vulnerable when governments try to reduce expenditures. In examining statistical agencies in developed countries around the world, Groves (2010, pp. 176) concludes, "One of the continuing challenges of statistical agencies is getting attention and support from the leaders who use their products, regardless of the sector of use." In the United States, "The Federal government typically spends between 0.15 and 0.40 % of its total budget on statistical activities, representing between $10 and $25 per year per resident for the country." (United States Office of Management and Budget 1999 to 2009). The high number for both of these series reflect the once a decade costs for the decennial census.

Pressure to limit government data collection is often highest when budgets are tight. But there is strong argument to be made that during times of budget cuts is exactly the wrong time to reduce the amount of data available for thoughtful decision making (Lewis and Burd-Sharps 2010).

Even though the cost of government data production is relatively small compared to other expenditures, statistical agencies have relatively few advocates outside of government. Moreover, many of the primary users of such data (scholars or researchers) are often not well organized to be active data advocates.

Given the low priority for data collection, advocates need to continually be a visible voice to promote the availability of data on children from government agencies and to make sure funds to support research on children are made available. In most cases such agencies are not in a good position to advocate for themselves and they need outsiders to represent the interests of data users. This is an opening for data-based advocates to "lobby" leaders to make sure government agencies have the resources they need to produce good quality data on children.

Getting government agencies to produce data that measures child well-being is not only useful in providing data to help us understand the well-being of children and the role of government assistance programs, I believe it helps elevate children on the public agenda. The importance of measuring child well-being is underscored by former Director of the United States Office of Management and Budget, Peter Orzag (2010, p. 34) who stated "Because what gets measured gets done". In other words, if a topic is not monitored on a regular basis it is easy for it to be overlooked.

A good example of data advocacy occurred in Ireland where the regular report on child well-being in their *State of the Nations Children* series spurred interest in developing additional data on children. In Ireland prior to the first publication of the State of the Nation's Children Report in 2006, very little data was published about the breadth of children's lives. Since the first publication *of State of the Nations Children* a number of Irish organizations, statutory and voluntary, have been active in publishing documents, reports and "report cards" on children's lives in Ireland. This is a welcome development and is possible because of the many improvements in data on children in Ireland over the last ten years. The quality of data has also been improved through interactions between the research unit and the various data holders, particularly those in service areas where the purpose of data collection is to support administrative tasks rather than to facilitate research.

Over the past few decades data advocacy has been successful in gaining several new sources of information. In the United States, the American Community Survey and the National Survey of Children's Health have emerged to provide more detailed data on child well-being. The development of Small Area Income and Poverty Estimates and the Small Area Health Insurance Estimates by the United States Census Bureau over the past 20 years is another example of expanded availability of data on child well-being.

Although this section is labeled more and better data, in recent times, many advocacy efforts in the United States have been focused on saving government data collections from being eliminated rather than advocating for more data. For example, House Bill H.R. 1638 introduced by United States Congressman Jeff Duncan in 2013 would have eliminated nearly all of the United States Census Bureau surveys, but data advocates were able to persuade other members of congress not to move forward on the bill.

Another example of losing ground is the publication called *Trends in the Well-Being of America's Children and Youth* that was published yearly by the U.S.

Department of Health and Human Services from 1997 to 2003. The publication provided nearly 400 pages of detailed data on children and youth, but publication was stopped in 2003, ostensibly for budgetary reasons. The point here is that advocates must remain vigilant not only to argue for addition data needed to provide a full portrait of child well-being, but to protect what is already available.

An example of where researchers have been instrumental in expanding the collection and provision of critical data is the emergence of several data collection efforts that provide comparable data across many countries. The provision of such statistical data not only has an impact in each country where country-specific data is provided, there is a collective impact that is achieved by enabling cross country comparisons. The importance of providing consistent standardized measures for countries is captured by UNICEF (2007, p. 3); "What is to be gained by measuring and comparing child well-being in different countries? The answer lies in the maxim 'to improve something, first measure it." A few such data collection and reporting efforts are discussed here. For more detailed information on comparable international surveys with data on children, see Brown et al. (2002).

The *Programme for International Student Assessment* (PISA) is a worldwide evaluation of 15-year-old school pupils' scholastic performance. The survey was first conducted in 2000, and then repeated every three years thereafter. It is coordinated by the Organisation for Economic Co-Operation and Development, with a view to improving educational policies and outcomes. More information about PISA is available on their website at http://en.wikipedia.org/wiki/Programme_for_International_Student_Assessment.

Another similar study is the Trends in International Mathematics and Science Study (TIMSS) which focuses on mathematics and science. TIMSS was first collected in 1995 and data have been collected several times since then. More information is available on their website at http://nces.ed.gov/timss/.

The *Health Behavior of School-Aged Children (HBSC)* study is a cross-national research survey conducted in collaboration with the World Health Organization Regional Office for Europe. The HBSC aims to gain new insight into, and increase the understanding of young people's health and well-being, health behaviors, and their social context. Initiated in 1982 in three countries, there are now more than 35 participating countries and regions. The first cross-national survey was conducted in 1983–1984, the second in 1985–1986, and subsequently every four years using a common research protocol. More information about HBSC is available on their website at http://www.nichd.nih.gov/about/org/despr/studies/behavior/HBSC.cfm.

In summary, advocating for more and better data on child well-being is an important activity in promoting child well-being and it is a goal shared by many scholars and child advocates. Over the past two decades there have been many successes in this endeavor, but also a few setbacks. The production of such data is not only important for gaining a better understanding of child well-being, but also because the absence of data on children or specific aspects of children's lives is likely to diminish the amount of public attention received. If the public is unaware of specific problems facing children they are unlikely to call for solutions to those problems.

2.4 Child Well-Being Monitoring

A key phrase used in child indicator world is "measuring and monitoring child well-being." The monitoring part of this phrase reflects on-going regular reports which allow users to see if child well-being is improving or deteriorating over time and/or to see if child well-being is better for one group of children than another. Monitoring suggests repetitive reports including the same measures of child well-being so progress, or lack of it, can be determined. Many of the reports discussed in previous sections provide this kind of monitoring capacity.

Scholars, advocates and communication experts, often have different views about the value of publishing a report every year. The different views are discussed in Appendix 2.

The production and use of child well-being indicators has expanded recently, in part, because they provide a useful way to determine whether a country, state, or group of children is moving in a positive or negative direction (Brown and Corbett 1997).

Many data-based child advocates understand the important role indicators and data play in monitoring. For example, Hood (2006, p. 249) concludes that "Monitoring and reporting on the well-being of children has a central role to play in the development of policies to improve children's lives." Brown and Moore (2009, p. 2) state, " Having strong data at the national and state level is key to developing, targeting, and monitoring policies and programs for children and youth."

Monitoring often involves using data for accountability. For example, one of the main purposes of *The Child Development Index* published regularly by Save the Children UK, (2013) includes "holding government to account for children's wellbeing" which is in the publication's subtitle. Likewise many provisions of the UNCRC invite on-going monitoring of child well-being from the children's rights perspective.

In summary, there are many examples of how data on children are being used to monitor developments over time. Such data provides an excellent way to determine if child well-being is improving or deteriorating

2.5 Goal Setting

Another use for statistical indicators of child well-being is their application in setting goals. Several examples of this type of application are described below.

In the United States, the federal government initiative called *Healthy People 2020* explicitly sets goals related to health and many relate to children. Some of the goals included in *Healthy People 2020* are:

- Reduce the rate of infant deaths,
- Reduce rate of child deaths,

- Reduce the rate of low weight and pre-term births,
- Increase the proportion of children who had access to a "Medical Home".

The articulation of such goals often helps shape policies to reach the goals and foster data collection needed to monitor movement toward the goal.

The *America's Children* report by the United States Inter-Agency Forum on Child and Family Statistics has played a similar role. After reviewing the use of the report, Bradburn and Fuqua (2010, p. 101) state, "This pegging of data to goals is one source of indicators power to engage and effect changes".

The America's Promise Alliance initiative in the United States has set a goal of increasing the high school graduate rate in the United States to 90 % by the year 2020. This goal helps drive the work of its alliance partners across the country (America's Promise 2013).

In Great Britain, a goal of cutting child poverty in half over ten years, lead to significant reduction in child poverty rates. There is widespread belief that identifying lower child poverty as a goal was crucial to the improvements in child poverty that were seen following adoption of the goal (Waldfogel 2010).

Millennium Development Goals set by the United Nations is another example were goal setting involved data and indicators. Many of the Millennium Development goals involve measuring and reporting on the well-being of children based on statistical indicators of child well-being.

In summary, using child indicators and statistical data on children to set and measure movement towards goals is another important part of data-based child advocacy.

2.6 Evaluating Programs and Policies

Indicators are increasingly seen as important to the policy process (Ben-Arieh and Frones 2009; Ben-Arieh and Goerge 2006). In discussing the changes experienced by the child indicators field in the past two decades, prominent child researchers Ben-Arieh and Goerge (2006, p.21) recently wrote;

> ...we argue that yet another change of focus is appropriate. We refer to the role of indicators in shaping policies and services, which requires that indicators be devised and used in ways that would extend their impact beyond building knowledge.

Many others agree. For example, one widely read European publication (Eurochild 2009) states;

> Indicators are increasingly valued as a means to interpret and present statistical data, monitor policy implementation, and provide the grounds for evidence-based policies and increased accountability.

This application of statistics on children fits neatly into the framework of data-based child advocacy.

Some would argue that major changes in governance over the past few decades have increased the relevance of child well-being indicators for policymakers. There has been more interest in public accountability over the past twenty years and this movement requires more and better data (Brown and Corbett 1997). In the United States context, Corbett (2008, p. 33) argues;

> In short, this focus on results, public accountability, and new forms of organizing social assistance increasingly demands a much more sophisticated use of what we broadly think of as social indicators.

Put succinctly, "Accountability requires counting." (The Annie E. Casey Foundation 2009b, p. 7). Counting (measuring) is the heart of the data-based child advocacy movement.

In the context discussed here, I argue that indicators are used in two different kinds of evaluation. The first kind is an evaluation of broad approaches to child welfare. For example, when countries or states are ranked in terms of child well-being, this is often taken as an evaluation of that country or that states' effort to care for children and is a reflection of a political regime or administration that holds power in that state or country. Assessing trends in child well-being over time is another way to assess the efficacy of political regimes or administrations and to hold leaders accountable for child well-being.

The study by Mekonen includes a Child Friendliness Index which is used to rank all 52 African countries based on the extent to which they have child friendly policies. Mekonen (2010, p. 207) defines a child-friendly government as "one which is making the maximum effort to meet its obligations to respect, protect, and fulfill child rights and ensure child well-being." The Global Movement for Children aspires to create a similar index for all countries in the world (Global Movement for Children 2010).

In the context of the United States, the devolution of program and policy responsibility from the federal level to the states has generated a need for more detailed measures of child well-being. As states have developed different approaches to public policies, evaluating the impact of those policies requires state-level data. The Assessing the New Federalism project collected data on child well-being from 13 states to assess varied state approaches to providing support for children and families. The work of the Assessing the New Federalism project can be found at http://www.urban.org/center/anf/index.cfm.

The second way in which indicators are used is in the evaluation of individual programs and policies. Statistical measures of child well-being are often used to determine whether a program has been a success or a failure. According to Ben-Arieh et al. (2001, p. 41);

> ....indicators make possible the evaluation of particular programs and policies, especially over time. Current policies can be examined in light of past efforts and evaluation of proposed changes can be enhanced.

There are many examples of how child indicators have been used in a public policy context (Belsky et al. 2006: Bernal 2008; Jack and Tonmyr 2008; Portwood et al. 2010; Rose and Rowlands 2010). The use of child indicators in a public policy context typically takes place at a national or state/provincial level, but they have also been used at the local level as well (McCroskey 2008).

In the United States, many researchers have used child indicators to show links between policy measures and overall child well-being in the states. For example Voss (1995) found that social service expenditures were very important predictors of child well-being across states. In another study, authors show that states with a higher tax rates (this reflects federal, state and local taxes paid by residents have better child outcomes than states with a lower tax rate (Every Child Matters Education Fund 2008). Another study found states that spend more on children have better outcomes (measured globally) even after taking into account potential confounding influences (Harknett et al. 2003).

Several scholars have found that more supportive state welfare policies are associated with better conditions and better outcomes for children (Cohen 1998; Ritualo and O'Hare 2000; O'Hare and Lee 2007; O'Hare et al. 2013b). Bradshaw and Richardson (2009, p. 319) examined several European countries and found;

> There are positive associations between child well-being and spending on family benefits and services and GDP per capita, a negative association with inequality and no association with prevalence of "broken" families.

In looking across developed countries, Bradshaw (2014) reports that the percentage GDP spent on families exhibits a positive correlation with subjective well-being among children, but the association does not rise to the level of statistical significance.

The 2009 Organisation for Economic Co-Operation and Development study of child well-being in developed countries devotes a chapter to examining the relationship between child well-being and social spending across the child's life cycle and another chapter to policy choices in early childhood (OECD 2009).The authors found substantial variation in social spending and public policies related to children across more developed countries.

One country where a child indicator report has been widely interwoven with government activities is Ireland. Several findings from the *State of the Nations' Children* report in Ireland related to gender differences in physical activities and a growing gender gap over time, resulted in a commitment by the Department of Health and Children (2000) to develop a national recreation policy for teenagers. The development of the recreation policy took place over a two year period and the policy "Teenspace—National Recreation Policy" was published in 2007.

One of the most important roles child indicators can play is in the rational or data-based distribution of public funds. For example, the United States government bases the distribution of several billion dollars in Education funding (Title 1) to states and school districts each year on the basis of child poverty rates. O'Hare (2012b) identifies six federal assistance programs that use measures of young children to distribute over $18 billion to states and localities each year.

Other researchers use specific child indicators in evaluation, such as using teen birthrates to evaluate the effectiveness of abstinence programs and test standardized test scores to evaluate education outcomes. Reflective of a number of similar reports, The Center on Education Policy (2011) used state-level standardized test scores in American public school students to assess educational attainment differences across states and among groups of students.

A number of organizations have assembled sets of child well-being outcome measures that can be used to assess education and training programs (Child Trends, undated) including some that attempt to assess the so-called soft skills, that have received increasing attention (Wilson-Ahlstrom et al. 2011).

In summary, child well-being indicators are being used in a variety of ways to assess policies and "policy-regimes." Such data are often used in an accountability context, that is, trying to hold leaders accountable for the general well-being of children.

References

America's Promise (2013). Building a Grad Nation Report: Progress and challenge in ending the High School Dropout Epidemic. http://www.americaspromise.org/Our-Work/Grad-Nation/Building-a-Grad-Nation.aspx.

Andrews, B. (2008). *Foreword in State of the Nations Children: Ireland 2008*. Ireland: Office of the Minister for Children and Youth.

Ben-Arieh, A., Kaufman, N. H., Andrews, A. B., Goerge, R. M., Lee, B. J., & Aber, J. L. (2001). *Measuring and monitoring children's well-being*. Dordrecht, Netherlands: Kluwer.

Ben-Arieh, A. (2006). Measuring and monitoring the well-being of young children around the world.In *Paper Commissioned for the EFA Global Monitoring Report 2007, Strong Foundations: Early Childhood Care and Education*.

Ben-Arieh, A., & Frones, I. (Eds.). (2009). *Indicators of children's well-being: Theory and practice in a multi-cultural perspective*. New York: Springer.

Ben-Arieh, A., & Goerge, R. M. (Eds.). (2006). *Indicators of children's well-being*. Dordrecht, Netherlands: Springer.

Ben-Arieh, A., & Gross-Manos, D. (2009). Taxonomy for child well-being indicators. In *Presentation at the 3rd Organisation for Economic Co-operation and Development, World Forum on "Statistics, Knowledge and Policy: Charting Progress, Building Visions, and Improving Life*. Busan Korea, Oct 27–30.

Belsky, J., et al. (2006). Effects of sure start local programmes on children and families: Early findings from a quasi-experimental cross sectional study. *British Medical Journal, 332,* 1476–1482.

Bernal, R. (2008). The effect of maternal employment and child care on child cognitive development. *International Economic Review, 49*(4), 1173.

Bradburn, N. M., & Fuqua, C. J. E. (2010). Indicators and the federal statistical system: An essential but fraught partnership. *The Annals of the American Academy of Political and Social Science, 631*, 89–108. Special editor Kenneth Prewitt.

-Bradshaw, J., & Richardson, D. (2009). An index of child well-being in Europe. *Child Indicators Research, 2*(3), 319–351.

Bradshaw, J. (2014). Overview: Social policies and child well-being. In A. Ben-Arieh, F. Casas, I. Frones & J. Korbin (Eds.), *Handbook of child well-being*. New York: Springer Publisher.

Brown, B. V., & Botsko, C. (1996). *A guide to state and local -level indicators of child well-being available through the federal statistical system*, Paper prepared for The Annie E. Casey Foundation, Baltimore, MD.

Brown, B., & Corbett, T. (1997). *Social indicators and public policy in the age of devolution.* Special Report No. 71. Madison: University of Wisconsin, Institute for Research on Poverty.

Brown, B. V., Smith, B., & Harper, M. (2002). *International Surveys of Child and Family Well-Being: An Overview.* Child Trends, Washington, DC.

Brown, B.V. ed. (2008). *Key Indicators of Child and Youth Well-Being: Completing the Picture,* Lawrence Erlbaum, Mahwah, NJ

Brown, B., & Moore, K. A. (2009). *What get measured get done: High priority opportunities to improve our nation's capacity to monitor child and youth well-being.* Child Trends, Washington, DC: Paper prepared for the Annie E. Casey Foundation.

Campaign for United States Ratification of the Convention on the Rights of the Child (2014). Information available on their website at http://www.childrightscampaign.org/.

Center for Education Policy. (2011). *State test score trends through 2008–2009: Progress lags in high school, especially for advanced achievers.* Washington, DC: Center on Education Policy.

Children's Institute, Berry, L., Biersteker, L., Dawes, A, Lake, L., & Smith C. (2013). *South african child gauge.* Cape Town: University of Cape Town. Available at http://www.ci.org.za/depts/ci/pubs/pdf/general/gauge2013/SouthAfricanChildGauge2013.pdf.

Child Trends (2011). Handout at the October 17, 2011. Washington, DC: Meeting of the Federal Interagency Forum on Child and Family Statistics Meeting.

Cohen, P. N. (1998).*State policies, spending, and kids count indicators of child well-being.* Washington, DC: Unpublished Paper by the Population Reference Bureau.

Corbett, T. J. (2008). Social indicators as a policy tool: welfare reform as a case study. In B. V. Brown (Ed.), *Key indicators of child and youth well-being: Completing the picture.* Mahwah, NJ: Lawrence Erlbaum.

Department of Health and Children (2000). *Our chidlren- their lives: The national children's strategy,* The Stationery Office, Dublin, Ireland.

Doek, J. E. (2014). Child well-being; children's rights perspective. In A. Ben-Arieh, F. Casas, I. Frones, & J. Korbin (Eds.), Handbook of child well-being. New York: Springer Publisher.

Eurochild (2009). *What are the latest policy developments at EU level.* Eurochild Policy Briefing No. 5, November, Brussels, Belgium.

Every Child Matters Education Fund (2008). *Geography Matters: Child Well-Being in the States,* Every Child Matters Education Fund, Washington DC.

Focus, First. (2013). *Children's budget 2013.* Washington, DC: First Focus.

Foundation for Child Development.(2013). *2013 child and youth well-being index (CWI).* Foundation for Child Development, New York. Available at http://www.fcd-us.org/sites/default/files/FINAL%202010%20CWI%20Annual%20Release.pdf.

Global Movement for Children (2010). *News release.* Available at http://www.gmfc.org/en/newsroom/gmc-press-releases-and-news/895-commitment-to-children-index-enters-new-phase.

Groves, R. M. (2010). The structure and activities of the United STATES federal statistical system: History and recurrent challenges. *The Annals of the American Academy of Political and Social Science, 631,* 163–179. Special editor Kenneth Prewitt.

Harknett, K., Garfinkel, I., Bainbridge, J., Smeeding, T., Folbre, N., McLanahan, S. (2003). *Do public expenditures improve child outcomes in the U.S.: A comparison across 50 states,* Princeton, NJ. Center for Research on Child Well-Being, Princeton University Working Paper 03-02.

Hood, S. (2006). Reporting on children's well-being: The state of London's children reports. *Social Indicators Research, 80,* 249–264.

Isaacs, J., Edelstein, S., Hahn, H., Toran, K., & Steurele, C. E. (2013). *Kids share 2013: Federal expenditures on children in 2012 and future projections.* Washington, DC: The Urban Institute.

Israel National Council for the Child Report (2007). *The State of the Child in Israel 2007: A Statistical Abstract.* Available at http://www.children.org.il/pro_articles_list_eng.asp?ProjectID=35.

Jack, S., & Tonmyr, L. (2008). Knowledge transfer and exchange: Disseminating Canadian child maltreatment surveillance findings to decision makers. *Child Indicators Research, 1*(1), 51–64.

Kilbourne, S. (1998). Opposition to United STATES Ratification of the United Nations convention on the rights of the child: Responses to parental rights arguments. *Poverty Law Journal, 4,* 56–112.

Lamb, V. & W.P. O'Hare (2013). Scalability of the CWI: State-level indicators and composite indices. In *chapter 7 in the Well-Being of America's Children: Developing and Improving the Child and Youth Well-Being* Index, Editor Kenneth C. Land.

Land, K. C., Lamb, V. L., & Mustillo, S. K. (2001). Child and youth well-being in the United States, 1975-1998: Some findings from a new index. *Social Indicators Research, 56,* 241–320.

Lewis, K., & Burd-Sharp, S. (2010). *The measure of America 2010-2011: Mapping risks and resilience.* New York, NY: New York University Press.

McCroskey, J. (2008). Using child and family indicators to influence communities and policy in Los Angeles County. In A., Ben-Arieh, & I. Frones (Eds.) (2009), *Indicators of children's well-being: Theory and practice in a multi-cultural perspective* (pp. 501–148). New York: Springer.

Mekonen, Y. (2010). Measuring Government performance in realizing child rights and child well-being: The approach and the indicators. *Child Indicators Research, 3*(2), 205–242.

National Conference of State Legislators (2004) . *State Legislators' Perceptions of KIDS COUNT,* National Conference of States Legislators, Denver, CO.

O'Hare, W. P., & Pollard, K. (1998). How accurate are state-level estimates from the current population survey? *Population Research and Policy Review, 17*(1), 21–36.

O'Hare, W. P, & Lee, M. (2007). *Factors Affecting State Differences in Child Well-Being,* KIDS COUNT Working Paper, The Annie E. Casey Foundation, Baltimore, MD. Available online at www.kidscount.org.

O'Hare, W. P. (2008). Measuring the impact of child indicators. *Child Indicator Research, 1*(4), 387–396, Springer.

O'Hare, W. P. (2012a). Development of the child indicator movement in the United States. *Child Development Perspectives, 6*(1), 79–84.

O'Hare, W. P. (2012b). *The Undercount of Children in the 2010 Census and Its Implications.* Paper Presented at the 2012 American Statistical Association Conference, San Diego CA.

O'Hare, W. P., Mather, M., Dupuis, G., Land, K. C., Lamb, V. I., & Fu, Q. (2013). Analyzing difference in child well-being among U.S . States. *Child Indicators Research, 6*(2), 401–431.

O'Hare, W. P., Riche, M., F., & Lippman, L. (2013) Development of the U.S. federal interagency forum on child and family statistics. In *Presentation at the 4th International Society for Child Indicators Conference,* Seoul, Korea. Available online at http://isci.chapinhall.org/wp-content/uploads/2013/06/P1_OHare_et_al.pdf.

Organization for Economic Co-Operation and Development (2009) *Doing better for children,* Chapter 2. Paris, France: Comparative Child Well-Being Across the Organization for Economic Cooperation and Development.

Orzag, P. (2010). Federal statistics and the policy making process. In *The Annals of the American Academy of Political and Social Science* (Vol. 631). Special editor Kenneth Prewitt.

Pollard, E. I., & Lee, P. D. (2003). Child well-being: A systematic review of the literature. *Social Indicators Research, 61,* 59–78.

Portwood, S. G. J, Shears, K., Eichelberer, C. N., & Abrams L. P. (2010). An institute for social capital: Enhancing community capacity through data sharing. *Child Indicators Research, 3*(2), 261–273.

Price, M. (2009). *Foreward in South African Child Gauge 2008/2009, Children's Institute* (p. 6). South Africa: University of Cape Town.

Red Por Los Derechos de la Infancia (2010). *La Infancia Cuenta,* Red Por Los Derechos de la Infancia. Mexico City, Mexico. Available at www.infanciacuenta.org.

Ritualo, A., & O'Hare, W. P. (2000). Factors related to state differences in child well-being. In Paper Presented at the Southern Demographic Association Conference.

Rose, W., & Rowlands, J. (2010). Introducing the concept of child well-being into government policy. In C. McAuley & W. Rose (Eds.), *Child well-being: Understanding children's Lives.* London: Jessica Kinglsey, Publishers.

Save the Children UK. (2012). *The Child Development Index: Holding Government to Account for Children's Wellbeing.* Save the Children UK, London. Available at http://www.savethechildren.org.uk/sites/default/files/docs/child-development-index.pdf.

Stagner, M., Goerge, R. M., & Ballard, P. (2008). *Improved indicators of child well-being.* Chicago: Chapin Hall at the University of Chicago.

The Annie E. Casey Foundation. (2005a). *County officials' perceptions and use of KIDS COUNT.* Available at http://www.aecf.org/KnowledgeCenter/Publications.aspx?pubguid={24D4E23B-A2E1-4428-88A1-85B3B0AB15B1}.

The Annie E. Casey Foundation. (2005b). *Business leaders' perceptions of KIDS COUNT.* Available at http://www.aecf.org/upload/publicationfiles/da3622h1256.pdf.

The Annie E. Casey Foundation. (2005c). *Summary of research findings: State legislative leaders' perceptions of KIDS COUNT.* Available at http://www.aecf.org/upload/publicationfiles/da3622h1261.pdf.

The Annie E. Casey Foundation. (2007). *Summary of research findings: Awareness, use and perceptions of KIDS COUNT among congressional staff.* Available at http://www.aecf.org/KnowledgeCenter/Publications.aspx?pubguid= {D92C23CA-7982-47C6-B74A-05464CF09057}.

The Annie E. Casey Foundation (2009a). Improve the nation's data on children and families, issue brief. Available at http://www.aecf.org/~/media/PublicationFiles/BriefDataDraft.pdf.

The, Annie E., & Foundation, Casey. (2009). *The KIDS COUNT data book.* Baltimore, MD: The Annie E. Casey Foundation.

The Annie E. Casey Foundation. (2011). *2011, KIDS COUNT data book.* Baltimore, MD: The Annie E. Casey. Available at http://datacenter.kidscount.org/DataBook/2010/Default.aspx.

UNICEF. (2007). *Child poverty in perspective: An overview of child well-being in rich countries,* Innocenti Report Card No. 7. Florence, Italy: UNICEF Innocenti Research Centre.

Untied Nations, (1989/1990*). United Nations convention on the rights of children.* Available at www.unhchr.ch/html/menu3/b/k2crc.htm.

United Nations. (2000). *United Nations Millennium Declaration.* Available at http://www.un.org/millenniumgoals/.

United Nations. (2014). *Every child counts.* New York, NY: United Nations.

United States Department of Education. (2013). *Literacy, numeracy, and problem solving in technology-rich environments among United States adults; results from the program for the international assessment of adult competencies 2012.* Washington, DC: National Center for Education Statistics.

United States Department of Health and Human Services (1980). *The status of children, youth, and families: 1979.* DHHS Publication No. (OHDS) 80-30274. Washington, DC: U.S. Department of Health and Human Services.

United States Office of Management and Budget (1999 to 2009). *Statistical programs of the United States Government; Annual Reports.* Washington, DC: United States Office of Management and Budget.

Voss, P. (1995). *Indicators of Child Well-being in the United States, 1985–1992: An analysis of related factors.* Baltimore, MD: The Applied Population Laboratory at the University of Wisconsin and The Annie E. Casey Foundation.

Vuckovic, S. N., Doek, J. E., & Zermatten, J. (2013). *The Rights of the Child in International Law. Rights of the Child in a Nutshell and in Context.* Bern: Stamlfli.

Wallman, K. K. (2011). Foreword to *America's Children: Key National Indicators of Well-Being, 2011.* Federal Interagency Forum on Child and Family Statistics, U.S Government Printing Office, Washington, DC. Page iii. Available online at http://childstats.gov.

Waldfogel, J. (2010). *Britain's war on poverty.* New York: Russell Sage Foundation.

Wilson-Ahlstrom, A., Yohalem, N., Dubois, D., & Ji, P. (2011). *From soft skills to hard data: Measuring youth program outcomes.* New York: The Forum for Youth Investment.

Chapter 3
Development of the Data-Based Child Indicator Movement

Table 3.1 shows some of the key events in the evolution of the data-based child advocacy movement, starting with the publication of the first United Nations report on the state of the world's children in 1979. The selection of 1979 as the starting point is somewhat judgmental. Clearly there were publications and reports on child well-being before 1979, but the volume, sophistication, and data-richness of such reports increased noticeably after 1979. In addition, the events and publications shown in Table 3.1 provide a sample of some of the kinds of activities that are part of the data-based child advocacy movement.

What explains the significant increase in data-based child advocacy since 1979? One answer was put forward in Chap. 1, where the unique situation of children with respect to political advocacy and the importance of increasing public awareness in a political context were discussed. But I think there is more. Data-based child advocacy has not developed in isolation. It is related to several other recent trends.

Some would argue that the increased interest in measuring the well-being of children is a reflection of increased public policy interest in children themselves (Statham and Chase 2010; Organisation for Economic Co-Operation and Development 2009). In talking about interest in the children in the United States, Gormley and Cymrot (2006, p. 102) state;

> We focused on child advocacy groups, which have become more conspicuous as children's' issues have attracted the interest of prominent politicians.

At the same time, it should be noted that the share of the United States Federal Budget that goes to support children has been shrinking. First Focus (2013, p. 3) found;

> Since a peak in 2010 total spending on children has fallen by $35 billion after adjusting for inflation, a 16 % drop. Total spending on children has declined 3 years in a row.

© The Author(s) 2014
W.P. O'Hare, *Data-Based Child Advocacy*,
SpringerBriefs in Well-Being and Quality of Life Research,
DOI 10.1007/978-3-319-07830-4_3

Table 3.1 Timeline of key events in data-based child advocacy/child indicators movement

Year	
1979	First United Nations State of the Worlds Children Report published
1980	
1981	First issue of Children's Defense Fund state report in United States published
1982	
1983	First Health Behavior of School-Aged Children Survey conducted
1984	
1985	
1986	
1987	
1988	
1989	United Nations adopts Convention on the Rights of the Child
1990	First KIDS COUNT report released in the United States
1991	
1992	First State of the Child in Israel published
1993	
1994	The United States Interagency Forum on Child and Family Statistics formed
1995	First round of United Nations Multiple-Indicators Cluster Survey launched
	First round of the *Trends in International Mathematics and Science Study* (*TIMSS*) conducted
1996	First meeting of the multinational project on measuring and monitoring child well-being—(Also known as the Jerusalem project because of where the first meeting took place)
1997	First United States Interagency Forum on Child and Family Statistics America's Children Report published
	Second meeting of the multinational project on measuring and monitoring child well-being held
1998	
1999	Third meeting of the multinational project held
2000	First Programme for International Student Assessment (PISA) survey conducted
2001	
2002	Second phase of multi-national project launched in Vienna
2002	Child Trends Data Bank launched in the United States
2003	Casey Foundation meeting of international data-based child advocates
2004	First issue of Foundation for Child Development Child Wellbeing Index published
2005	

(continued)

Table 3.1 (continued)

Year	
	Oslo conference on childhood included a special track on child indicators and launching of the International Society for Child Indicators
	First "La Enfancia Cuenta" report published in Mexico
2006	International Society for Child Indicators (ISCI) is formed
2007	First ISCI international conference (held in Chicago, USA)
	Child well-being in the European Union Report Published
2008	First Issue of *Child Indicators Research* journal published
	Child well-being in the CEECIS published -Wikichild first produced
2008	The Annie E. Casey Foundation convenes first meeting of data-based child advocates in Latin America
2009	Second ISCI conference (held in Sydney, Australia)
2010	
2011	Third ISCI conference (held in York, England)
2012	
2013	Fourth ISCI conference (Held in Seoul, Korea)

In another study, Bradshaw (2014) found that the United States was the only one of 22 developed countries he studied were government expenditures per child as a percent of GDP decreased from 1980 to 2007.

So if indeed there has been increased attention to children in the United States it does not seem to be reflected in increased resources from the federal government. Others report that children seldom get their fair share of attention in political discussions. Bruner and Chencar (2011) report that only 2 % of the time in the early presidential debates in the primaries prior to 2012 United States Presidential election was devoted to discussion of children's issues.

There is a symbiotic relationship between data-based child advocacy and several larger worldwide movements or trends discussed below. The data-based child advocacy movement gains from these trends and contributes to them as well. The extent to which data-based child advocacy is intertwined with so many other developments suggests that it will also continue to grow as other trends continue. Five trends which are connected to the rise of data-based child advocacy are discussed below in no particular order.

First, data-based child advocacy is part of the increased attention to social measurement and social indicators. In many ways measurement has been the foundation of the scientific developments that have dramatically changed most societies over the past century. Over the 20th century there was a sustained interest in measuring almost every aspect of human life (Hicks and Wattenberg 2001). The social indicators movement in the 1960 and 1970s, which is often discussed as a pre-cursor to the child indicators movement, is part of that long term trend (Brim 1975a, b). Lippman (2005) provides a good history of the child indicator movement in the United States. The widespread development of report cards on children and other regular reporting of measures of child well-being reflect this measurement movement (Pollard and Lee 2003; Ben-Arieh 2006). The social indicators movement and particularly the child indicator movement, is closely related to the rise of data-based child advocacy (Ben-Arieh 2008). The data-based child advocacy movement is part of an effort which is pushing governments and researchers to measure and monitor the human condition more robustly and more regularly than ever before.

The child indicators movement and the data-based child advocacy movement are closely related by not completely overlapping. There are some aspects of the child indicator movement that are almost exclusively focused on advancing scholarship rather than advancing child well-being and vice versa.

Second, data-based child advocacy adds its voice to those asking for a less economic-centric way of measuring human progress (Stiglitz et al. 2009; Thiry et al. 2013). Critics say that statistics such as Gross National Product have driven decision-making for too long and that such economic-driven statistics do not reflect real human progress. The movement can be seen as part of a move to define human success and/or human or social progress in terms other than money (Leon and Boris 2010). In recent years many terms like "Quality of Life", "Happiness", "Life Satisfaction", etc. have emerged as preferential concepts for assessing human progress which reflects movement away from a purely monetary view of well-being.

The typical approach to measuring child well-being is not focused on an economic perspective. With 114 chapters, the recent *Handbook of Child Well-Being* reflects the multi-dimensional concept of child well-being (Ben-Arieh et al. 2014). Indices of child well-being typically take a multi-dimensional view of child well-being (O'Hare and Guttierrez 2012).

Third, the rise of data-based child advocacy is related to the increased interest in government and social accountability. Data-based child advocacy is closely related to several governance ideas such as "results-based accountability", "results based governance" or "data-based decisions making", that have become more visible recently (Friedman 2005; Wandersman et al. 2000; Skalski and Romero 2011).

The fourth trend is the increase in the use of data for decision-making. Many data-based child advocacy reports are clearly meant to encourage decision-makers to use scientific data for decision making rather than basing policy decisions on ideology, politics, myths, or other non-scientific basis. One data-based child advocate (Friedman 2005, p. 12).concludes;

> If we rely just on impressions and anecdotes, we really don't know if things are getting better or worse. By using common sense measures, we can be honest with ourselves about whether or not we are making progress.

The Annie E. Casey Foundation (2009, p. 1) perspective is captured in a line for a publication a few years ago: "Good decisions are based on good data, and a hallmark of the Casey Foundation's approach to helping children and families succeed is using sound data to advocate for change".

Fifth, the emergence of data-based child advocacy is related to the growth of what is often called "translational research". This refers to attempts to be more systematic and more intentional about getting facts and scientific knowledge into the hands of political decision-makers (Clark et al. 2013). This is an effort to bridge producers and consumers of scientific evidence and promote the utilization of research in a public policy or public interest context (Hutchinson 1995; Lester 1993). The bridging nature of data-based child advocacy fits neatly into the translation research model.

One such effort in the United States is called the Family Impact Seminar. Their website describes its purpose as;

> The Policy Institute for Family Impact Seminars aims to strengthen family policy by connecting state policymakers with research knowledge and researchers with policy knowledge.

More information about the policy institute for the family impact seminars is available at http://familyimpactseminars.org/.

Another kind of "translational research" can be found in *The Future of Children* publication series which begin in the early 1990s. The Future of Children website (http://futureofchildren.org/futureofchildren/publications/journals/) describes the initiative;

> Because The Future of Children aims to reach a wide audience with the best objective research possible, our articles are literature reviews. They provide a balanced view of the evidence, review both basic and "policy-relevant" research, and avoid using overly technical language.

In Europe, the Eurochild network has a similar aim of bridging research and policy. The activities of Eurochild, according to its website, are listed below and many activities fall into my definition of data-based child advocacy. More information about Eurochild is available at http://www.eurochild.org/.

- Sharing information on policy and practice
- Monitoring and influencing policy development at national and European level
- Creating interest groups and partnerships between member organizations
- Representing the interests of its members to international institutions
- Strengthening the capacity of its members through training, individual advice and support.

I believe there may be an additional reason why data books and report cards filled with statistics on child well-being have expanded so much over the past few decades, at least in the United States socio-political context. I think this type of report appeals to both conservatives and liberals. For conservatives these types of reports offer measurement and accountability. Some conservatives are drawn to data-based reports on children because they often provide the same kinds of data that businesses find useful for decision-making. Liberals often feel that data books are documenting the kinds of problems and issues they would like to have government address.

The increased interest in data-based child advocacy as I define it here is also reflected in the evolving organizational infrastructure. Recent increases in use of child indicators is closely related to the emergence of the International Society for Child Indicators (ISCI), an organization where scholars, researchers, advocates, and data users can discuss issues of conceptualizing, measuring, and reporting and use of child well-being indicators.

After several informal/ad hoc meetings of child indicator experts from the mid-1990s onward, ISCI was formally organized in 2006. ISCI now has a journal (*Child Indicator Research*), a book series, a regular newsletter, and the organization has sponsored four international conferences. The rapid rise of ISCI reflects widespread interest in this field.

The stated goals of ISCI are; (see http://www.childindicators.org/goals.html)

- Contribute to the well-being of all children.
- Share knowledge and experience.
- Develop standards.
- Improve data resources.
- Foster collaborative research and projects.
- Foster diversity in methodological approaches.
- Enhance dissemination of information on the status of children.
- Help organizations apply the findings to policy and practice.
- Enhance the capacity of the field in countries that are in the initial stages of producing child well-being indicators.

Many of goals put forth by ISCI go beyond scholarship into realms of advocacy particularly in communicating results and applying indicators to policy and practice.

Child Indicators Research, the professional journal of the International Society for Child Indicators began publication in 2008. Since then the number of manuscripts submitted for publication has grown systematically from 24 in 2008 to 85 during 2012 and 84 in 2013 (see Fig. 3.1). The upward trajectory is pretty clear and the increased number of submissions reflects growing interest in this field.

Broad interest in data on children is reflected in the readership of the *Child Indicators Research* journal. The impact score from *Child Indicators Research*, 0.864 in 2012, is very high for a new journal. For those who may not be familiar with an impact score, the definition is offered by Wikipedia (http://en.wikipedia.org/wiki/Impact_factor),

The *impact factor* (IF) of an academic journal is a measure reflecting the average number of citations to recent articles published in the journal. It is frequently used as a proxy for the relative importance of a journal within its field, with journals with higher impact factors deemed to be more important than those with lower ones.

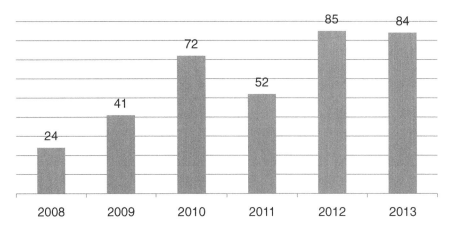

Fig. 3.1 Number of manuscripts submitted to *Child Indicators Research* Journal: 2008–2013

I believe that a robust organizational infrastructure is critical for any successful movement and the emergence of ISCI helps promote a more rapid advancement in data-based child advocacy.

There is an odd juxtaposition of data-based child advocacy activity and recognition of the concept of data-based child advocacy. Despite the proliferation of child well-being data and reports over the past few decades there are few articles in the scholarly or popular literature clearly focused on the use child indicators in an advocacy context.

A perusal of several recent textbooks on child indicators did not find a single article or chapter with word "advocacy" in it (Ben-Arieh and Frones 2009; Ben-Arieh et al. 2001; Ben-Arieh and Goerge 2006; Brown 2008; Hauser et al. 1997; Naar-King et al. 2004) Although the word "advocates" appeared in one article, little information in the article is focused on use of data by advocates (Moore and Brown 2006).

While many of the articles in the text books cited above and articles in the *Child Indicators Research* journal are linked to advocacy-related activities (for example, by linking indicators to public policies) none couch their narrative as advocacy per se. Examination of the first 24 issues of the journal *Child Indicator Research* found only two articles with the word "advocacy" or "advocate" in the title. One by Rasmusson (2011), focused on centers in Sweden where children suspected of being exposed to sexual or physical abuse, rather than the use of child indicators in an advocacy context. Another article by O'Hare (2013) describes the KIDS COUNT project in the United States. Examining the keywords associated with all of the articles in the first 24 issues of *Child Indicator Research* showed that none used the word "advocate" or "advocacy".

ISCI has sponsored four international conferences since 2007. Looking at the presentations made at the four ISCI conferences that been held since 2007, I found only two papers with the word "advocacy" and "advocate" in the title (Rasmusson 2009; Carrasco et al. 2011).

The recently released *Handbook on Child Well-Being* (Ben-Arieh et al. 2013) is a signature achievement in terms of covering topics related to child well-being. It includes 114 chapters in five volumes, but only one chapter (O'Hare 2014) is explicitly focused on the use of data in a child advocacy context. It should be noted, however, several chapters contain elements of data-based child advocacy. For example, one chapter focuses on social policies (Bradshaw 2014), two chapters focus on the United Nations Convention on the Rights of the Child (Lundy 2014; Mekonen and Tiruneh 2014). Other chapters such as "A Framework for Action" (Leadbeater et al. 2014) and "Measuring the Effects of Child Welfare Interventions" (Aizer and Doyle 2014) focus on topics related to data-based child advocacy.

Lists of how child well-being indicators are used seldom mention advocacy. For example, Brown and Corbett (1997) list five uses of social indicators but use as an advocacy tool is not one of the five. Reidy (2011) also provides a list of how child indicators are used, but does not include advocacy. Weil (2001) list three main ways in which data and research are used but does not call any of them advocacy even though some of the purposes he lists, such as shaping the policy agenda, could easily be labeled advocacy.

Articles from a child indicator perspective do not cover use in child advocacy, and typically articles from a child advocacy perspective do not address the use of child indicators or data in an advocacy context (Takanishi 1978; Knitzer 2005; Dalrymple 2005).

In summary, even though there is widespread use of statistical data in child advocacy activities, there is a dearth of written information explicitly focused on the use of child indicators in an advocacy context. This gap may be due, at least in part, to how advocacy is defined and perceived. One of the obstacles to recognizing the use of child indicators in advocacy is the narrow view of advocacy. De Vita et al. (2001, p. 4) state, "The term 'advocacy' is often considered synonymous with "lobbying" but such a narrow definition captures only one function in a much broader set of advocacy activities". As I define data-based child advocacy, many child indicator experts and scholars are already more involved in advocacy activity than they may recognize.

It is also important to recognize that advocacy does not necessarily mean adversarial. Many times advocacy involves recognizing and working with allies or other groups that have a common interest. It can also involve helping other individuals or groups that have a goal of promoting child well-being, for example, by providing data.

The lack of articles on the advocacy uses of data on children may also be due in part of the relative newness of the data-based child advocacy activities and the difficulty in defining the term or recognizing the commonality among various segments of the movement.

The data-based child advocacy movement has been somewhat difficult to identify and define because it involves so many different types of professionals and organizations from numerous arenas. It has been fostered and enhanced by work in philanthropy (O'Hare 2009; Foundation for Child Development 2013; Global Movement for Children 2010), international organizations (UNICEF 2013; Organisation for Economic Co-Operation and Development 2009), government agencies (The United States Interagency Forum on Child and Family Statistics 2013; Irish Minister for Health and Children 2008), civil society (Save the Children UK 2013; Steketee et al. 2012), nonprofit research organizations (Child Trends 2013), and academia (Stagner et al. 2008).

In addition, the development of the data-based child advocacy movement has been driven by a diverse mix of scholars, scientists, researchers, policymakers, journalists, advocates, and practitioners. The growth of the data-based child advocacy movement has involved many different scholarly disciplines such as sociologists, psychologists, demographers, social workers, statisticians, lawyers, public policy experts, and many others. This rich mix of providers and users and the breadth of organizations involved often mean this work does not fit neatly into existing frameworks and it is not always easy to see the commonality across efforts.

Another reason data-based child advocacy has not been widely recognized is that data-based child advocacy activities are often very limited in a given community, state, or country. But collectively such activities can be seen as a new social force. I believe the information in this publication will convince readers that data-based child advocacy is growing and that it represents an opportunity to combine research and scholarship with activities designed to improve the lives of children.

The breadth of data-based child advocacy has a cost and a benefit. The variety of forms and contexts of data-based child advocacy make it more difficult to identify and define, but the fact that this approach is being reflected in so many different disciplines and contexts suggest that it has wide applicability.

In summary, the data-based child advocacy movement has gained momentum in recent decades, in part, because it is intertwined with and closely related to several other trends, particularly the child indicators movement. Although the use of data in advocacy contexts has increased in recent decades there is little recognition in the professional literature of this trend, at least using the term "advocacy". The lack of recognition may be due, at least in part, to the diverse set of actors and settings involved in data-based child advocacy.

References

Aizer, A., & Doyle, J. J. (2014). Economics of child well-being: Measuring effects of child welfare interventions. In A. Ben-Arieh, F. Casas, I. Frones, & J. Korbin (Eds.), *Handbook of child well-being*. New York: Springer.

Ben-Arieh, A. (2006). Measuring and monitoring the well-being of young children around the world. *Paper commissioned for the EFA global monitoring report 2007, strong foundations: Early childhood care and education.*

Ben-Arieh, A., Kaufman, N. H., Andrews, A. B., Goerge, R. M., Lee, B. J., & Aber, J. L. (2001). *Measuring and monitoring children's well-being.* Dordrecht, Netherlands: Kluwer.

Ben-Arieh, A., & Goerge, R. M. (Eds.). (2006). *Indicators of children's well-being.* Dordrecht, Netherlands: Springer.

Ben-Arieh, A. (2008). The child indicators movement: Past, present, and future. *Child Indicators Research, 1*(1), 3–16.

Ben-Arieh, A., & Frones, I. (Eds.). (2009). *Indicators of children's well-being: Theory and practice in a multi-cultural perspective.* New York: Springer.

Ben-Arieh, A., Casas, F., Frones, I., & Korbin, J. (Eds.). (2014). *Handbook of child well-being.* New York: Springer.

Bradshaw, J. (2014). Overview: Social policies and child well-being. In A. Ben-Arieh, F. Casas, I. Frones, & J. Korbin (Eds.), *Handbook of child well-being.* New York: Springer.

Brim, O. G. (1975a). Macro-structural influences on child development and the need for childhood social indicators. *American Journal of Orthopsychiatry, 45*(4), 516–524.

Brim, O. G. (1975b). Childhood social indicators: Monitoring the ecology of development. *Proceedings of the American Philosophical Society, 119*(6), 119–125.

Brown, B., & Corbett, T. (1997). *Social indicators and public policy in the age of devolution.* Special report no. 71. Madison: University of Wisconsin, Institute for Research on Poverty.

Brown, B. V. (Ed.). (2008). *Key indicators of child and youth well-being: Completing the picture.* Mahwah, NJ: Lawrence Erlbaum.

Bruner, D. C., & Chencar, B. (2011). *Moving America's children into the spotlight: The presidential election as an opportunity for dialogue about America's Children* Child and Family Policy Center, Des Moines, IA.

Carrasco. S., Villa, R., Ponferrada, M., & Casanas, E., (2011). Child participation: A model for child advocacy. Paper presented at the 3rd ISCI conference York England.

Clark, F., Park, D. J., & Burke, J. P. (2013). Dissemination: Bringing translational research to completion. *The American Journal of Occupational Therapy, 67*(2), 165–193.

Child Trends. (2013). *The youngest Americans: A statistical portrait of infants and toddler in the United States.* Washington, DC: Child Trends.

Dalrymple, J. (2005). Constructions of child and youth advocacy: Emerging issue in advocacy practice. *Children and Society,19*, 3–15.

De Vita, C. J., Mosher-Williams, R., & Stengel, N. A. J. (2001). Nonprofit organizations engaged in child advocacy. In C. J. De Vita & R. Mosher-Williams (Eds.), *Who speaks for America's children? The role of child advocates and public policy* (pp. 3–38). Washington DC: The Urban Institute Press.

First Focus. (2013). *Children's budget 2013.* Washington, DC: First Focus.

Foundation for Child Development. (2013). *2010 child and youth well-being index (CWI).* Foundation for Child Development, New York. http://www.fcd-us.org/sites/default/files/FINAL%202010%20CWI%20Annual%20Release.pdf

Friedman, M. (2005). *Trying hard is not enough: How to produce measurable improvements for customers and communities.* Victoria, Canada: Trafford Publishing.

Global Movement for Children. (2010). *News release.* http://www.gmfc.org/en/newsroom/gmc-press-releases-and-news/895-commitment-to-children-index-enters-new-phase

Gormely, W. T., & Cymrot, H. (2006). The strategic choices of child advocacy groups. *Nonprofit and Voluntary Sector Quarterly, 35*(1), 102–122.

Hauser, R. M., Brown, B., & Prosser, W. (Eds.). (1997). *Indicators of children's well-being.* New York: Russell Sage Foundation.

Hicks, C. T., & Wattenberg, B. J. (2001). *The first measured century.* Washington, DC: The AEI Press.

Hutchinson, J. (1995). A multimethod analysis of knowledge use in social policy. *Science Communication, 17*(1), 90–106.

Irish Minister for Health and Children. (2008). *State of the nation's children: Ireland 2008.* Dublin, Ireland: Department of Health and Children, The Stationery Office.

Knitzer, J. (2005). Advocacy for children's mental health: A personal journey. *Journal of Clinical Child and Adolescent Psychology,34*, 612–618.

Leadbeater B., Mitic, W., & Egilson, M. (2014). Monitoring the health and well-being of developing childen in changing context: A framework for action. In A. Ben-Arieh, F. Casas, I. Frones, & J. Korbin (Eds.), *Handbook of child well-being*. New York: Springer.

Leon, E., & Boris, E. T. (2010). *The state of society: Measuring economic success and human well-being*. Washington DC: The Urban Institute.

Lester, J. P., (1993). The utilization of policy analysis by state agency officials. *Knowledge Creation, Diffusion and Utilization, 14*(3), 267–290.

Lippman, L. (2005). *Indicators and indices of child well-being: A brief history*, KIDS COUNT Working paper. Baltimore: Annie E. Casey Foundation. Retrieved July 17, 2011, from http://www.aecf.org/KnowledgeCenter/Publications.aspx?pubguid = {74238176-1D59-4043-AA9A-E9FFC72CCC2C}

Lundy, L. (2014). United nations convention on the rights of the child and child well-being. In A. Ben-Arieh, F. Casas, I. Frones, & J. Korbin (Eds.), *Handbook of child well-being*. New York: Springer.

Mekonen, Y., & Tiruneh, M. (2014). Implementation of the convention on the rights of the child and its effect on child well-being. In A. Ben-Arieh, F. Casas, I. Frones, & J. Korbin (Eds.), *Handbook of child well-being*. New York: Springer.

Moore, K. A. & Brown, B. V. (2006). Preparing indicators for policymakers and advocates. In A. Ben-Arieh, & R. M. Goerge (Eds.), *Indicators of children's well-being: Understanding their role, usage, and policy influence*. Dordrecht, The Netherlands: Springer.

Naar-King, S., Ellis, D. A., & Frey, M. A. (2004). *Assessing children's well-being: A hand book of measures*. Mahwah, NJ: Lawrence Erlbaum.

O'Hare, W. P. (2009). The role of philanthropy in indicators development and use. Paper presented at the organization for economic cooperation and development conference in Busan, South Korea, October 2009. http://www.Organization for Economic Cooperation and Development.org/site/progresskorea/44124304.pdf

O'Hare, W. P., & Guttierrez, F., (2012) The use of domains in constructing a comprehensive composite index of child well-being. *Child Indicators Research, 5*(4), 609–630.

O'Hare, W. P. (2013). A case study of data-based child advocacy: The kids count project. *Child Indicators Research,6*(1), 33–52.

O'Hare, W. P. (2014). Data-based child advocacy. In Ben-Arieh, F. Casas, I. Frones, & J. Korbin (Eds.), *Handbook of child well-being* (pp 3043–3067). New York: Springer.

Organisation for Economic Co-Operation and Development. (2009). *Doing better for children*, Chapter 2, Comparative child well-being across the organization for economic cooperation and development. Paris, France: Organisation for Economic Co-Operation and Development.

Pollard, E. I., & Lee, P. D. (2003). Child well-being: A systematic review of the literature. *Social Indicators Research,61*, 59–78.

Rasmusson, B. (2009). Children's advocacy centres in Sweden, experiences of children. Presentation at the 2nd ISCI conference, Sydney, Australia

Rasmusson, B. (2011). Children's advocacy centres (Barnhaus) in Sweden. *Child Indicators Research,4*(2), 301–322.

Reidy, M. (2011). *Key themes: Reflections from the child indicators projects—General uses of child indicators studies*, report to United STATES Department of Health and Human Services. http://www.aspe.hhs.gov/hsp/cyp/child-ind98/keythemes/gen-uses-of-ind-studies.htm

Save the Children UK. (2013). *Surviving the first day: State of the worlds mothers 2013*. London, England: Save the Children UK.

Skalski, A. K.,& Romero M. (2011). Data-based decision making. *Principal leadership*. National Association of Secondary School Principals, January.

Stagner, M., Goerge, R. M., & Ballard, P. (2008). *Improved indicators of child well-being*. Chicago: Chapin Hall at the University of Chicago.

Statham J., & Chase, E. (2010). *Child wellbeing: A brief overview*. Loughborough University, Childhood Wellbeing Research Centre.

Steketee, M., Mak, J., & Tieroff B. (2012). *Kinderen in Tel Databoek 2012* (rough translation KIDS COUNT Data Book 2012). The Netherlands: Verwey-Jonker Institute.

Stiglitz, J. E., Sen, A., & Fitoussi J. P. (2009). *Report by the commission on the measurement of economic performance and social progress.* Retrieved July 17, 2011, from www.stiglitz-sen-fitoussi.fr

Takanishi, R. (1978). Childhood as a social issue: Historical roots of contemporary child advocacy movements. *Journal of Social Issues,34*(2), 8–28.

The Annie E. Casey Foundation. (2009). *The KIDS COUNT data book.* Baltimore, MD: The Annie E. Casey Foundation.

The United States Interagency Forum on Child and Family Statistics. (2013). *America's children: Key indicators of child well-being.*http://www.childstats.gov/americaschildren/

Thiry, G., Bauler, T., Sebastien, L., Paris, S., & Lacroix, V. (2013). *Characterizing demand for beyond GDP.* Final report of BRAINPool, European Commission.

UNICEF. (2013). *The state of the world's children: 2013.* New York, NY: United Nations Children's Fund.

Wandersman, A., Imma, P., Chinmanb, M., & Kaftarianc, S. (2000). Getting to outcomes: A results-based approach to accountability. *Evaluation and Program Planning,23*, 389–395.

Weil, A. (2001). *Uses of data and research*, assessing the new federalism, The Urban Institute, Washington DC.

Chapter 4
Communication Issues

Communication is such a fundamental part of data-based child advocacy that I decided to devote a separate Chapter to the topic. A good communication strategy is critical for effective data-based child advocacy and often this means using mass media, such as newspapers, television, radio, and perhaps social media to disseminate data and findings. In addition, good data-based child advocacy often means statistical experts and communication experts must work together. After reviewing news media and child well-being, Carter (2014, p. 1979) concluded, "The news media are central agents in the advancement of children's well-being in democratic societies".

Data is a particularly powerful tool because it can be used to reach both a policy-making audience and a broad segment of the public. According to Richard King (2014, p. 33) policy research advisor to OXFAM, "In terms of advocacy and making your case to the public and to the people who make decisions—yes, a lot of that is based on understanding the data."

The reason communication is such an important topic for data-based child advocates is captured by a statement from the Organisation for Economic Co-operation and Development (2008, p. 8); "When good statistics exist, they too often go unnoticed or misunderstood by a broad audience." In other words, producing good data is not enough to ensure that the data are used or used properly. In order to reap the maximum benefits of investment in conducting research or gathering data they must be shared with others. Among scholars, sharing often occurs through professional publications and professional conferences, but such sharing of information and ideas seldom reaches elected officials, decision makers, or the broader public.

Many data-based child advocates see two distinct ways in which coverage in the mass media can have an impact on policy. First, popular media are used to influence elected officials and their staffs directly because public officials often monitor news coverage.

© The Author(s) 2014
W.P. O'Hare, *Data-Based Child Advocacy*,
SpringerBriefs in Well-Being and Quality of Life Research,
DOI 10.1007/978-3-319-07830-4_4

Second, mass media are also used to try and sway public opinion. Reaching a broad audience is important because in democracies, publically elected officials generally respond to the issues raised by the people who elect them—the public. A review of the literature by American Association of Public Opinion Research (2013, p. 11) concluded;

> An extensive research literature shows noticeable responsiveness and congruence between public opinion and policy decisions, indicating that basic democratic processes are at work.

Studying the impact of widespread public news coverage Barabas and Jerit (2009) also concluded;

> We show how the volume, breadth, and prominence of news media coverage increases the policy-specific knowledge above and beyond common demographic factors.

These studies indicate that news coverage does have an effect on policy-makers, at least to the extent that it increases their knowledge on issues.

To the extent data-based child advocates can move children's issues higher on the public agenda by providing good information on child well-being through mass media the more likely publically elected officials are to seek public policy solutions to the problems facing children. A report on state legislators and child advocacy in the US (State Legislative Leaders Foundation 1995, p. 13) acknowledged this point and concluded;

> ...the leaders do acknowledge that media coverage can influence public opinion, which in turn, prompts legislators to act on issues that otherwise might have remained untouched.

Using mass media to get information into the hands of policymakers and public audiences is also seen as a way to leverage what are often scare resources in the child advocacy world. In their discussion about disseminating important data on children in Canada, Jack and Tonmyr (2008, p. 51) conclude;

> Extensive resources are invested in the production of research with the anticipation that relevant findings will be understood and utilized by decision-makers to inform practice and policy.

Another reflection on this issue is offered by Axford et al. (2013, p. 161) who concluded, "Lots of child well-being data is collected but is rarely exploited fully." Many others echo this point (Lester 1993; Hutchinson 1995; Dunn and Holzer 1988). Reaping the full benefits of data-based reports and research often requires strategic use public or mass media.

The heavy use of the mass media by child advocates is consistent with Gormley's (2012) view that child advocates need to rely on an "outsider strategy" which was discussed in Chap. 1. Gormley believes child advocates have little influence working directly with elected officials and their staffs (largely because children don't vote and child advocates have little money to devote to political campaigns) so they must lean heavily on trying to use information to mobilize constituents to put pressure on elected officials.

It is important to understand and appreciate the situation of the audience(s) you are trying to reach, but there is a fair amount of confusion about information flows to elected officials or other public decision-makers. One view of the communication context for public officials is provided by Anderson and Harbridge (2013, p. 1) as;

> Information in the political world is not scarce. Policymakers are bombarded by signals from constituents, from lobbyists, from Dear Colleague Letters, and from many other sources of information that offer conflicting messages.

But analysis by the Kellogg Foundation (no date) suggests good information is not always easily available to decision-makers;

> As a result, today's state policymakers can find themselves in a double bind. They need timely accurate information, such as objective analysis related to social issues more than ever before, but they have less time to seek information and more difficulty finding it.

A report by the State Legislators Leaders Foundation (1995, p. 11) from a few years ago, concluded;

> Only a few legislative leaders express familiarity with current research related to children and families,

The different views about communication and elected officials are often not so much about the volume of information flowing to elected officials but the kinds of information flowing. The statement "drowning in statistics but starved for information," captures a related idea.

However, many decision-makers indicate they are relatively satisfied with the data they already have available. Over 80 % of a representative sample of state legislators and their aides (National Conference of State Legislators 2004) said they were "very satisfied" or "somewhat satisfied" with data currently available for tracking the status and well-being of children in their state. Likewise, 72 % of representative sample of United States Congressional aides (The Annie E. Casey Foundation 2007) indicated that they were "very satisfied" or "somewhat satisfied" with data that are currently available at the federal level for tracking status and well-being of children.

This suggests that it may not be a lack of data that is holding back positive policy and programmatic changes for children. It may be the way the data are packaged or delivered that is not influential. Or it may be that elected officials are not ready or willing to act until they feel action is demanded from their constituents. Some evidence reviewed below suggests that constituents may not be as well informed on children's issues as elected officials.

Given the uncertain communication situation regarding getting information to public officials, thoughtful planning is critical. Discussions about good communication often involve "strategic communications." This term means different things to different people but one organization (The Annie E. Casey Foundation 2003, p. 2), defines strategic communication as;

The processes by which data are transformed into information, and then knowledge, knowledge is translated into messages, and messages are tailored and delivered to multiple audiences in a way that effectively equips them to support children and youth in their own realms, and so that young people can advocate and make decisions on their own behalf.

I am not tied to this particular definition of strategic communications, but I think it highlights the complexity involved in designing and executing a good communication plan. It is not simple, and often not cheap.

Many scholars and advocates share the goal of getting information about child well-being into the hands of political leaders and decision makers. The California child advocacy organization Children Now (2003, p. 3) conclude, "Getting their issues into the hands of top decision-makers is an ongoing job for most advocates, with many investing significant resources into grabbing the media's attention."

Among advocates, it is widely believed that getting information into newspapers helps elevate their issues on the public agenda. Many elected officials, at least in the United States, pay close attention to what is covered by the major newspapers in their region or districts. A report by the child advocacy group California Now (2003), found state policymakers in California still used newspaper more than any other source for news and this point is also acknowledged by state legislators (State Legislative Leaders Foundation, 1995).

The Congressional Management Foundation (2011) asked congressional aides about what influences member's views, and 75 % said newspaper editorial endorsement on an "issue" had "a lot" or "some" influence. However, it should be noted that there were seven other strategies that aides rated higher than a news editorial endorsement in terms of potential influence. Moreover, this question is limited to editorial endorsement and does not include regular newspaper coverage of an issue or group.

Some people take the view that what issues are discussed in the media is more important than exactly what is said about those issues. In talking about the press, Cohen (1963) said, "It may not be successful much of the time in telling people what to think, but it is stunningly successful in telling its readers what to think about." This is consistent with the "Agenda Setting" ideas that have been discussed in communications and political science work for many years (McCombs 1993; McCombs and Shaw 1972).

In discussing this issue with one prominent United States child advocate, Michael Petit head of the Every Child Matters Child advocacy organization, he stated, "We already know a lot about what needs to be done to increase the well-being of children, what we need is the political will to implement what we know works." From this perspective what is needed is communication to make the issue of child well-being more salient to elected officials and other leaders and to move it higher on the public agenda rather than communication about specific policy solutions.

But using popular media to communicate facts and statistics about children is not always successful. Newspaper stories about children often lack quantitative data (Kunkel et al. 2002; Haaga 2003). One study (O'Hare 2003) found that only

39 % of stories related to children in five major United States newspapers over the course of a year contained statistical data.

The dearth of statistical data in newspaper stories about children may help explain why a large share of the public lacks accurate statistical knowledge about children. A survey which asked a representative sample of American adults about several dimensions of child well-being, found that there were often large differences between the public's perception and the official data. Guzman et al. (2009) found, for example, less than half the adults could correctly select the child poverty rate from three alternatives. Only 5 % of adults knew roughly what percent of children in the United States lacked health insurance. Moreover, when adults held misperceptions about the state of child well-being, they tended to accentuate the negative (Guzman et al. 2009; The Public Agenda 1997).

Such misperceptions are not confined to the United States. Similar misperceptions were found in England (Jakens 2008) and in Latin America. According to the Inter-American Development Bank (2008, p. 1), "People's perceptions are often in stark contrast to reality; compared to objective indicators, opinions in some countries are too optimistic and others too pessimistic." Such misperceptions underscore the need for more media coverage of regular fact-based reports on children.

In the context of data books or report-card type publications, numerous attempts have been made to make the data available in alternative forms to try and reach as broad an audience as possible. To some extent, different audiences prefer different products. Table 4.1 shows a number of these types of "spinoffs" products from datebooks' or report cards that organizations have used to try and extend the reach of their publications. Since the costs of gathering the data is fixed, such spinoffs help gain a bigger return on investment.

Data-based child advocacy often requires that scholars and researchers communicate with audiences other than other scholars and researchers (Li 2011). Trying to reach the public with data-focused messages presents a unique set of problems (Leibovitz 2007).

Public audiences differ from academic audiences on two key points. First, academic colleagues usually read articles on children because they are already interested in the topic. On the other hand, public audiences are not necessarily interesting in child well-being, so the writer must capture their interest. Second, academic audiences are comfortable with science and statistics, but a large segment of the pubic are not convinced by science and are uncomfortable with statistics.

The three quotes below are meant to be humorous, but they also capture an element of how a significant segment of the public views statistics.

There are three kinds of lies; lies, damn lies, and statistics" Author Mark Twain

Statistics are like a bikini: what is revealed is interesting, but what is concealed is vital" Author Unknown

Table 4.1 Alternative mechanisms for disseminating data from reports

A variety approaches have been used by different initiatives with the aim of enhancing the dissemination and/or visibility of indicator reports and to "extend the brand." Several of these are listed below
(1) Data Wheel—a hard cardboard wheel where one can spin the inner wheel to reveal child well-being indicators for each state or country
(2) Pocket Guide—a 3 by 8 inch foldout that provides data for all States or countries
(3) Wall Chart—a 2 feet by 3 feet wall chart with key data on child well-being for all States or countries
(4) State or country specific data sheets—one or two pages with key information for each state or country.
(5) Release event—an event to highlight the release of a report
(6) Video News Release—short video clips prepared in advance that can be released on the data as a report is made public… good for gaining TV coverage
(7) Local release events in selected locations—linking the main release with staged events in selected localities around the country
(8) E-readers format—As devices such as Nooks and Kindles become more popular, some initiatives are releasing reports in e-reader format
(9) Use of graphics Infographics
(10) Use of Social Media…. Mobile Apps, Facebook, twitter accounts etc
(11) Produce a Brief rather than a full report every other year

There are two kinds of statistics: The type you look up and the type you make up. Author Unknown

The distrust of statistical evidence among a large segment of the public reflected in these quotes poses a challenge for data-based child advocates.

Most researchers have little or no training in using the mass media or public communication strategies and I am sure some researchers feel that getting information to the public or to policymakers is not their job. On the other hand, in my experience many scholars would like to see their research findings have more impact on public awareness and public policies. And organizations that publish data books or report cards would like to see their data used by decision-makers.

Education in social science or statistics seldom provides the kind of exposure to public communication skills or strategies that are needed for successful data-based child advocacy (Starbuck 2013). The description by Berg (2013, p. 18) below is focused on statisticians, but I think it applies to many quantitatively trained social scientists,

Although the acquisition and application of statistical skills is a necessary step in achieving success as a professional statistician, it is not sufficient. One also must develop the ability to influence customers, colleagues, managers and subordinates. This can be especially problematic when those you are trying to influence are not statistically savvy and you must convince them of the merits of a particular statistical approach.

To the extent scholars and researchers want their work to influence public attitudes or public policy, using mass communication is often critical.

Combining good scientific data and communication expertise in reaching a mass audience can be vexing to participants because it often involves a clash of cultures between data experts and communication experts. For example, scholars strive for abstractions and generalities, but communication with the public often works best when one gives specifics. To give a quick example, scholars want to describe the characteristics of states or countries that have high levels of child well-being but communication experts want to list specific states or countries with the best or worst levels of child well-being. Identifying a state or country as first or last in a ranking has enormous communication power with the popular press but ranking is seldom used in scholarly analysis. To provide another example, scholarly work typically includes a lot of caveats and cautions about the results. In writing meant for non-scholars, caveats and cautions are often seen as undermining the veracity of the results of the report.

Table 4.2 provides a summary of some key differences between writing for scholarly colleagues and writing for non-scholarly audiences.

A quick scan of the differences shown in Table 4.2, highlight potential problems when scholars or researchers try to work with communications experts. However, it is important to point out that these differences are not insurmountable. There are lots of examples, including many reviewed in this publication, which show one can combine good data practices and good communication skills in one publication.

Some of the most perplexing issues or challenges regarding combining good social science research and good communication practices in a data book or report card type publication are discussed in more detail in Appendix 2.

In terms of communication I feel I should say something about the rise of social media and the internet. But with respect to social media, it is so new and it is changing so rapidly that I am not sure there is very good evidence yet with respect to its impact on data-based child advocacy. Perhaps all that can be said is that it is growing rapidly and data-based child advocates should monitor it and use it when appropriate.

The internet has had a big impact on how data and studies get distributed. Fifteen to 20 years ago, the primary way data on child well-being was made available to the public was through printed matter. To some extent, the role that was played by printed products 20 years ago is now being filled by web-based applications (McNutt 2007). Researchers, analysts, journalists and others have quickly moved from relying exclusively on printed products to relying more and more on the internet.

Clearly, the use of the internet to disseminate information is on the rise. According to former Chief Statistician at the OECD, Giovannini (2008, p. 1) states; "The development of web 2.0 and other Information and Communication Technologies (ICT) are creating a revolution in the way in which information is produced and shared among different interest groups and individuals." Both statistical data and studies or reports are now widely available on the internet. Many examples of that are given in Tables 2.1 and 2.2 and URLs sprinkled through this publication.

Table 4.2 Key differences in writing for scholars and writing for non-scholars

Issue/topic	Writing for a scholarly audience	Writing for a non-scholarly audience
Use of Jargon	Technical jargon is often used and expected in scholarly reports	Technical jargon should be minimized or terms should be clearly explained if used
Simple and User Friendly	This is not necessary in scholarly writing. It is assumed that readers are already interested in and knowledgeable about the topic	Critical in writing for the public. One should not assume that the reader is familiar with the topic and/or is automatically interested in it. One has to engage the reader
Use easily understood measures	Not necessary in scholarly writing. Scholars can be expected to spend the time needed to understand whatever measures are being used	Critical in writing for the public. If readers have any difficulty understanding the measures they are likely to stop reading
Use of Public Media	Seldom used in scholarly publications	Often used in advocacy publication… including a press release, and prepping authors for interviews from reporters
Producing regular updates	Scholars seldom replicate past work, they build on it	Many advocacy reports are produced regularly to increase visibility and allow monitoring of changes over time
Localizing/ personalizing information	Names of countries, state, or cities are seldom given. Scholars are more likely to give the characteristics of a state rather than the name of the state. For generating generalizable results the specific state is not important	Use of specific places can generate local interest and expand media coverage of a report
Timeliness of data	In scholarly publications this is seldom a high priority. Moreover, the peer review and publication process almost guarantee the data in an article will not be the most recent available	For the public, and particularly for policymakers, having the most recent data is critical. Elected officials who don't like the findings from a study can easily dismiss them if the statistics are outdated
Lead with findings	Findings are often put at the end of the report after theory, data and methods and analysis have been discussed. Readers of scholarly reports can typically be counted on to read to the end	Key findings are put early in the report and often are in the title. Many readers of advocacy reports may only read the title or first part of the report
Detailed methodology	Scholars are expected to provide a detailed description of their methodology	Most readers of advocacy reports are not equipped to assess detailed social science methodology. Methodological descriptions should be minimized and/or put in an appendix

(continued)

Table 4.2 (continued)

Issue/topic	Writing for a scholarly audience	Writing for a non-scholarly audience
Credibility	Credibility is derived from using good scientific methods	Credibility is derived from the credibility of the individual or organizations producing the report and/or the spokesperson(s) recruited to deliver the message

Note this table is based, in part, on a presentation by Stephen Tordella of Decision Demographics

The cost of making data available through the internet is often much cheaper than making it available through printed publications. In discussing a major data collection and dissemination project Leibovitz (2007, p. 6) concluded, "For example, electronic communications proved an effective way to reduce cost of printing and mailing publication and put materials in the hands of stakeholders faster." Another example involves The Annie E. Casey Foundation. In the 1990s the Foundation spent $300,000–$400,000 a year to print 50,000–60,000 *KIDS COUNT Data Books*. Now that cost is greatly reduced because much of the data that used to be in the printed report is available from the Foundation on their website.

The internet not only offers an opportunity to provide more data to users at a relatively cheap cost, it also provides an opportunity to get available data to users faster than through printed reports. In web-based delivery, one does not have to wait for a yearly publication to make data available. Websites can be updated regularly. Given the value of timeliness, this is an important consideration.

The movement from printed products to web-based dissemination as raised questions about the best way to disseminate data-based reports. Printing and mailing reports are expensive, particularly when reports are large as they often are with data books. While dissemination on the web is typically cheaper, many believe that some key audiences (such as older elected officials) still prefer a printed report. Organizations have had to make difficult decisions about how much effort and money to put into print versus online dissemination efforts. Although there are many good reasons for focusing on web-based dissemination, some professionals feel there is still something useful about having a hard-copy to give to select audiences.

Over the past quarter century, as data-based child advocacy has developed, there have been parallel changes on the media side. For example, the Journalism Center on Children & Families at the University of Maryland was established in 1993 to foster more and better news coverage of child and family issues. According to their website the Center, "inspires and recognizes exemplary reporting on children and families, especially the disadvantaged." More information is available at their website: http://www.journalismcenter.org/about/mission-and-vision.

There have also been advances among journalist with respect to use of data. The rise in the combination of data analysis and newspaper reporting as given rise to data-based reporting as a separate brand of journalism. The headline of a recent story in the popular United States newspaper USA TODAY (Yu 2014) reads "Data-driven journalism soars."

The National Institute for Computer-Assisted Reporting (NICAR) is a program of Investigative Reporters and Editors, Inc. and the Missouri School of Journalism. Since 1989, NICAR has trained thousands of journalists in the practical skills of getting and analyzing electronic information and also maintains a library of databases containing government data on a wide array of subjects, available for purchase by Investigative Reporters and Editors members. More information is available at their website http://www.ire.org/nicar/.

In summary, communication is critical for successful data-based child advocacy. But most data experts have little or no training in using mass media or communicating with non-scholars. Successful data-based child advocacy often requires merging data expertise and communication expertise, but these two groups often have different norms.

References

Anderson, A., & Harbridge, L. (2013). *The policy consequences of motivated information processing among partisan elite, working paper series*, *WP-13-02*, Evanston, IL: Institute for Policy Research, Northwestern University.

Association of Public Opinion Researchers. (2013). Polling and Democracy: *Report of the AAPOR Task Force on Public Opinion and Leadership*.

Axford,N., Hobbs, T. & Jodrell, D. (2013). Making child well-being data work hard: Getting from data to policy and practice, *Child Indicators Research*, *6*(1), 161–178.

Children Now. (2003). *Children now media alert*, May 13, 2003, Oakland, CA: Children Now.

Barabas, J., & Jerit, J. (2009). Estimating the causal effects of media coverage on policy-specific knowledge. *American Journal of Policy Science*, *53*(1), 73–89.

Berg, P. H. (2013). Influence: Essential for success as a statistician. *AMSTAT News, The Membership Magazine of the American Statistical Association*, Issue # 435, September.

Carter, C. (2014). News media and child well-being. In:A. Ben-Arieh, F. Casas, I. Frones & J. Korbin (Eds.), *Handbook of child well-being*. Berlin: Springer.

Cohen, B. (1963). *The press and foreign policy*. Princeton, NJ: Princeton University Press.

Congressional Management Foundation. (2011). *Communicating with congress: Perceptions of citizens advocacy on capitol hill*. Washington, DC: Congressional Management Foundation.

Dunn, W., & Holzer, B. (1988). Knowledge in society: Anatomy of an emergent field. *Knowledge in Society*, *6*, 6–26.

Giovanninni, E. (2008). *The role of communication in transforming statistics into knowledge, organisation for economic co-operation and development, paper presented at the conference innovative approaches to turning statistics into knowledge*. Sweden May: Stockholm. 2008.

Gormley, W. T. (2012). *Voices for children: Rhetoric and public policy*. Washington, DC: Brookings Institution Press.

Guzman, L., Lippman, L., Moore, K. A. O'Hare, W. P. (2009). Accentuating the negative: The mismatch between public perception of child well-being and official statistics. *Child Indicator Research*, *2*, (4), 391–416.

Haaga, J. (2003). Why Didn't You Write What I Thought I Said? *Paper delivered at the Population Association of America Conference*, May.

Hutchinson, J. (1995). A multimethod analysis of knowledge use in social policy. *Science Communication, 17*(1), 90–106.

Inter-American Development Bank. (2008). *Beyond the facts: Understanding quality of life, ideas for development in the Americas* (Vol. 17). Washington, DC: Inter-American Development Bank.

Jack, S., & Tonmyr, L. (2008). Knowledge transfer and exchange: Disseminating canadian child maltreatment surveillance findings to decision makers. *Child Indicators Research, 1*(1), 51–64.

Jakens, F. (2008). Media Stereotypes are alienating a whole generation argues Felix Jakens, *Compass; direction for the democratic left*. http://www.compassonline.org.uk/news/item.asp?n=3473.

Kellogg Foundation. (No date). *The challenge of informing all state policy Makers*. From a Presentation at Michigan State University in October 1998, Kellogg Foundation, Battle Creek, MI.

King, R. (2014). A life in statistics. *Significance, 11*(1), 33–36.

Kunkel, D., Smith, S., Suding, P. & Biely, E. (2002). *Coverage in context: How thouroughly the news media report five key children's issues*, Study Commissioned by the Casey Journalism Center on Children and Families, Philip Merrill College of Journalism. MD: University of Maryland, College Park.

Leibovitz, H. (2007). *Dissemination lessons learned*. Assessing the new federalism. Washington, DC: Urban Institute. Retrieved from http://www.urban.org/publications/411502.html.

Lester, J. P. (1993). The utilization of policy analysis by state agency officials. *Knowledge Creation, Diffusion and Utilization, 14*(3), 267–290.

Li, J. (2011). *Child Indicators: Lost in Translation*, presentation at the International Society for Child Indicators Conference, York, England. Retrieved online from http://isci.chapinhall.org/wp-content/uploads/2011/09/Li-Junlei.pdf.

McCombs, M. E., & Shaw D. L. (1972). Agenda-setting function of mass media. *Public Opinion Quarterly, 36*, 2.

McCombs, M. E (1993). The evolution of agenda-setting research: Twenty-five years in the marketplace of ideas. *Journal of Communication, 13*. 2.

McNutt, J. G. (2007). Adoption of new wave electronic advocacy techniques by nonprofit child advocacy organizations. In M. Cortes & K. Rafter (Eds.), *Nonprofits and technology: Emerging research for usable knowledge*. Chicago, IL: Lyceum Books.

National Conference of State Legislators. (2004*). State legislators' perceptions of KIDS COUNT*, National Conterence of States Legislators, Denver, CO.

O'Hare, W. P. (2003). *Perceptions and misperceptions of America's children: The role of print media*, KIDS COUNT Working Paper, The Annie E. Casey Foundation, Baltimore, MD.

Organization for Economic Cooperation and Development. (2008). *Global project on measuring the progress of society towards a strategic action plan*. Paris, France: STD/CSTAT, Organization for Economic Cooperation and Development.

Starbuck, R. (2013). Communicating with clients AMSTAT NEWS, Issue 437, November, pp 25–26.

State Legislative Leaders Foundation. (1995). *State legislative leaders: Keys to effective legislation for children and families, a report*. Centerville, MA: State Legislative Leaders Foundation.

The Annie E. Casey Foundation. (2003). Data-based advocacy. Baltimore, MD: The Annie E. Casey Foundation.

The Annie E. Casey Foundation. (2007). *Summary of research findings: Awareness, use and perceptions of KIDS COUNT among congressional staff*. Retrieved from http://www.aecf.org/KnowledgeCenter/Publications.aspx?pubguid={D92C23CA-7982-47C6-B74A-05464CF09057}.

The Public Agenda. (1997). *Kids these days: What Americans really think about the next generation*. New York: The Public Agenda.

Yu, R. (2014). Data-Driven Journalism Soars. *USA Today, 17*, 4b.

Conclusions

I am convinced that data-based child advocacy is growing around the world and has enormous potential to increase global child well-being. Today hundreds of individuals and dozens of groups are using data to improve the lives of children and the number of people and groups involved in this activity grows every year. Data-based child advocacy has been growing because it has become an effective tool to help child advocates and researchers reach their goals of getting good data into the hands of users and improving child well-being.

Because data-based child advocacy involves a variety of methods and a wide mix of individual and organizational actors, commonality of the work and the connections across approaches are not always apparent. To date, the collective nature of this work as data-based child advocacy has often been overlooked. Despite the rapid increase in use of child indicators and the expressed interest of many scholars to see that their work has an impact, there is a dearth of articles or publications about the use of child indicators in an advocacy context. While child advocacy activities are not widely recognized within the child indicator research community, many people are already engaged in some forms of data-based child advocacy.

I believe there are ample opportunities for scholars to participate in advocacy activities in ways that do not compromise their scientific principles using a data-based child advocacy approach. I also believe that many child advocates can make more effective use of data within the data-based child advocacy framework. The continued and expanded use of child indicators and a greater appreciation for their use in advocacy contexts will likely give the concept of data-based child advocacy more visibility over the next few decades.

I hope readers of this publication who see their work as primarily about improving child welfare will gain a better appreciation for the value of good statistical data and those who see they work as primarily scholarship or research can better see how their work connects with child advocacy. While advocacy and social science are often seen as distinct fields, the framework provided by data-based child advocacy provides an opportunity for professionals in these two fields to work together to improve the quality of life for children.

© The Author(s) 2014
W.P. O'Hare, *Data-Based Child Advocacy*,
SpringerBriefs in Well-Being and Quality of Life Research,
DOI 10.1007/978-3-319-07830-4

Appendix 1
Data-Based Child Advocacy in Latin America

In 2002, The Annie E. Casey Foundation in the United States (AECF) convened an international "learning exchange" where leading child advocates, researchers and government officials from Canada, Chile, Ireland, Israel, Jordan, Mexico, the Netherlands, and the United Kingdom shared their different approaches to data-based child advocacy. A relationship developed through this exchange with the Children's Rights Network in Mexico/Red por los Derechos de la Infancia (REDIM) which sparked the exportation of the KIDS COUNT data-based advocacy model to Mexico and more recently to other countries in Latin America. This article summarizes recent child indicator work that has developed in Brazil, Paraguay, Chile and Nicaragua with support from AECF and REDIM.

Background

KIDS COUNT, a project of the Annie E. Casey foundation, is described in Chap. 2 of this publication. Child advocates in the United States and increasingly from around the world view this model as a useful tool to protect children and their rights.

KIDS COUNT staff began working with the Children's Rights Network in Mexico/Red por los Derechos de la Infancia (REDIM) in 2003 to replicate the KIDS COUNT model in order to measure and protect children's rights in Mexico. REDIM published an analysis of data available in 2004 and their first KIDS COUNT/Infancia Cuenta report in 2005, a report that has since been published on an annual basis (http://www.infanciacuenta.org/). Their work and presentations of their work at Red Latino Americana y Caribeña por la Defensa de los Derechos de los Niños, Niñas e Adolescentes/Latin American and Caribbean Network for the Defense of Children and Adolescents (REDLAMIC) and other regional meetings sparked interest across many countries in Latin America to use the KIDS COUNT model as a tool to ensure governments comply with The United Nations Convention on the Rights of the Child.

© The Author(s) 2014
W.P. O'Hare, *Data-Based Child Advocacy*,
SpringerBriefs in Well-Being and Quality of Life Research,
DOI 10.1007/978-3-319-07830-4

In 2008, 2010, 2011, and again in 2013, the Annie E. Casey Foundation and REDIM convened children's rights advocates interested in incorporating the data-based advocacy model into their efforts, including representatives from Argentina, Chile, Brazil, Mexico, Nicaragua and Paraguay, in order to share experiences and gain technical assistance in the areas of data, communications and policy advocacy. The technical assistance and support provided through these meeting have allowed organizations to obtain the knowledge necessary to start developing and implementing the KIDS COUNT model into their work. Momentum continues to grow.

The most recent of these meetings, held in Mexico City in November 2013, demonstrated the progress many of these organizations have made in advancing the quality of data-based child advocacy in their respective countries and illuminated areas that need improvement. For example, despite limited funding, since 2011, Mexico and Brazil continue to produce annual data-books focused on the well-being of children and adolescents in their countries while Paraguay and Chile have produced their first data-books. Paraguay and Chile both noted the successes of their launches and are currently seeking funding to produce a subsequent report.

While each country may be in a different state with regard to advancing the quality of data-based advocacy, they each highlighted strong commonalities of barriers they face in their work. For example, although child advocates from Mexico, Brazil, Chile, Nicaragua, and Paraguay have legal precedence to conduct their work via a human rights approach (each respective nation has signed the Convention on the Rights of the Childwhich formalized a political system and process for the protection of children and adolescents) they each note that they face the difficult task of cultivating a data-based decision making culture in their work and throughout society. Efforts to promote data-based decision making range from weaving data with youth voice in advocacy in Mexico to providing training to journalists in Nicaragua to ensure reporting of the highest quality. Ensuring that data is presented in a usable and easily understandable way has proved a difficult task.

Additionally, all participants noted a need for technical assistance with their online data presentation capacities. Many countries, such as Brazil, distribute their data-books via hard copy and compact disk. In the case of Brazil, the data-book can range up to 300 pages. To more efficiently and effectively inform the public on the well-being of children, these child advocates are beginning to explore website platforms to disseminate their work, akin to the KIDS COUNT Data Center (http://datacenter.kidscount.org/). Interestingly, all participants noted the need to incorporate local universities and academics in their work. Unlike the United States, Latin American advocates highlighted that working with academics and universities is key to establishing the credibility of the child-advocacy movement in Latin America. Chile, for example, partners with the University of Chile to advance their data-based advocacy work.

The summary below highlights recent reports produced in Brazil, Paraguay, Chile and Nicaragua that are modeled after AECF's KIDS COUNT project and

REDIM's *Infancia Cuenta* work. These child indicator reports fill a void in the measurement world and provide governments, advocates and citizens with the tools to protect the rights of children where they live.

Brazil

The National Forum for the Defense of Children and Adolescent Rights (NFDCAR) is a coalition of 56 diverse organizations that work together with 27 state councils to protect the rights of children in Brazil. The Forum produced the first child indicator report for Brazil in 2011 with funding from the Marista Solidarity Network/RedeMarista de Solidariedade (RMS) that works to promote and protect children's rights. In 2012 they released their second child indicator report *Where are the Children Brazil—2011/CADÊ Brasil—2011*, which includes data for the 27 States in Brazil. The report includes data for 59 indicators in the areas of demographics, citizenship, health, education, housing, economy, justice, child participation, legislation.

These reports filled a void, making data available as a tool to advocates and policymakers to measure, strengthen and protect the rights of children and adolescents. The state of Paraná recently contacted NFDCAR and asked them to produce a local child indicator report for their state and 399 municipalities. NFDCAR is expecting to receive more of these requests as localities realize the power of data for decision-making. Access report online at: www.solmarista.org.br.

Since 2009, The National Forum for the Defense of Children and Adolescent Rights have held workshops for monitoring child and adolescent well-being indicators throughout various states. In addition, they played an advisory role in the recent development of the national budget, which provided them with a unique opportunity to promote a child and youth agenda.

Paraguay

The Coalition for Childhood and Adolescent Rights Paraguay/Coordinadorapor los Derechos de la Infancia y la Adolescencia Paraguay (CDIA), is an association of 31 non-governmental member organizations that promote and defend children and adolescent rights in Paraguay. Through their Observatory (CDIA Observa), they have developed an indicator system to monitor Paraguay's compliance with the Convention on the Rights of the Child. The Observatory is responsible for collecting and disaggregating data relating to the well-being of children in Paraguay.

They developed their first indicator report in 2011 titled, *Kids Count Paraguay, Indicator system for Children and Adolescents. Data Book/La Infancia Cuenta Paraguay, Sistema de Indicadores en Niñez y Adolescencia. Libro de Datos.* Using roughly 36 indicators, this report paints a picture of how children are faring at the national- and department-level in the areas of demographics, economic well-being, health, education, citizenship, protection and provides recommendations on how the nation can best protect the rights of their children. In 2012 CDIA traveled the country, educating their constituents (i.e. government officials using data presented in the report) and building their case for making children's rights central to government decision making. In addition to producing physical copies of the report, CDIA has an online portal where they post Infancia Cuenta, articles, legislative results and the outcomes of their projects and work. As a result of this work, CDIA has cultivated some strong relationships with government agencies, including the Ministry of Education. In fact, since the release of the first data-book, the national assembly has requested a subsequent report. Access report online at: www.cdiaobserva.org.py.

Chile

El Observatorio Niñez y Adolescencia (Child and Youth Observatory) promotes and generates significant knowledge about the situation of children and adolescents in Chile, through periodic reports and thematic research on public policy, children's rights and adolescence. In May, 2013, The Child and Youth Observatory released their first report, *Violencia contra Niños, Niñas y Adolescente,* (violence against children and adolescents) which analyzes public data, from a rights perspective, on poverty, rural, indigenous landownership and overcrowding. To produce this report, the Child and Youth Observatory partnered with UNICEF Chile, The University of Chile, and the Marista organization. After popular demand, the Child and Youth Observatory is currently seeking funding for a second report and are developing a comprehensive metric-scale to evaluate the outcomes of future work. Access report online at: http://issuu.com/observatorioninezchile/docs/informe_violencia

Nicaragua

Established in 1992, La Federación Coordinadora Nicaragüense de ONG quetrabajan con la Niñez y la Adolescencia (CODENI) is a group of 37 organizations and agencies that promote public policies to improve the lives of children and youth in Nicaragua. To achieve these goals, CODENI influences public policy, proposes laws, engages in social advocacy and employs strategic communications. CODENI is a member of 'Coordinadora Sub-Regional' or the Sub-Regional Coordinator (El Salvador is currently the Secretary of the Sub-Regional Coordinator) which consists of Guatemala (CIPRODENI), Panama (H.S.I.), Nicaragua (CODENI), Mexico (REDIM), El Salvador (RIA), Dominican

Republic (NGO Coalition for Children), Costa Rica (COSECODENI) and Honduras (COIPRODEN). The Sub-Regional Coordinator allows participants to collaborate to elevate the field of child advocacy in the region and serves as a platform for members to more effectively monitor the well-being of children.

Within the past year, CODENI has established an Observatory on the rights of children and adolescents in Nicaragua. The Observatory is an online tool that contributes to the defining, implementation and evaluation of public policies and public and private actions that protect the rights of children and youth. The site includes publications, newsletters, alerts and news updates.

This Observatory is focused on the monitoring and evaluation of public policies, as well as the behavior and communication of the state of the rights of children and adolescents taking into account the rights established in the policy of the Constitution, the code on children and adolescents and the Convention of the Rights of the Child. The Observatory uses indicators known as 'national instruments' which include: child health, early childhood education, child nutrition, and social protection and 'international instruments' which are outlined in the Convention on the Rights of the Child. The Observatory also includes socio-demographic data at the national level like population, birth rate, etc.

Conclusion

The adoption of the KIDS COUNT data-based advocacy model by the Children's Rights Network in Mexico in 2003 spurred interest across Latin America in data-based child advocacy. This article highlights the most recent reports produced in Brazil and Paraguay and Chile. We recognize that this summary represents only a sample of the data-based advocacy work in Latin America but we feel it provides a flavor of what is happening in the region with respect to data-based child advocacy.

Signed

Florencia Guttierrez and Ketih Calix

The Annie E. Casey Foundation

Appendix 2
Some Key Questions Regarding Data-Based Child Advocacy Publications

There are several issues that come up repeatedly in producing data-based child advocacy reports. These often pit the approach of researcher and data analyst with the approach of communication experts. I address some of these issues below in the form of questions. For most of these questions there is not a single clear answer.

Should Statistical Significance Testing be Used?

Scholars are typically taught to test differences (differences between two points in time, or differences between geographic units, or differences between groups) to establish the probability that the observed difference could be due to chance. This is called statistical significance testing. But statistical significance testing is seldom used in data-based child advocacy publications even though they are fraught with the kinds of differences described above. An examination of 25 articles that used comprehensive domain-driven indices of child well-being found that none of them employed statistical significance testing (O'Hare 2012).

Statistical significance testing has been a very valuable tool for scientists for a long time but from a communication point of view, adding information about statistical significant to a data book "clutters" the presentation. This is particularly true in publications where there are a multitude of comparisons. For example, in the 2013 *KIDS COUNT Data Book* there are sixteen indicators of child well-being and a combined overall index of well-being for each of the 50 States. Showing tests of statistical significance for all possible comparisons would add a large number of additional figures or notations to an already packed presentation. And for many readers statistical significance tests may be more confusing that clarifying. In addition, it is not clear that many readers would understand statistical significant testing (Child Trends 2002).

While statistical significance has been crucial for science, it may not be the right criteria for making decisions in a public policy context. In that context I think it is informative to examine what levels of uncertainty are used in other arenas like the courts, media, and legislators.

© The Author(s) 2014
W.P. O'Hare, *Data-Based Child Advocacy*,
SpringerBriefs in Well-Being and Quality of Life Research,
DOI 10.1007/978-3-319-07830-4

The use of statistical significance testing is perhaps the biggest difference between use of child indicators in work intended to increase public awareness and use in work intended for a scholarly audience.

What is an Indicator of Child Well-Being?

The selection of indicators of child well-being is a critical part of data-based child advocacy but exactly what is an "indicator of well-being?" In the context of data-based child advocacy it is important to understand the distinction between *statistics* and *indicators*. Nearly all indicators of child well-being are statistics but not all statistics are indicators of child well-being.

Some statistics are useful for gaining a better understanding of children but may not be seen as indicators of child well-being. For example, describing the age composition, the racial composition, and perhaps the geographic distribution of children is often useful, but these statistics typically don't provide information on well-being.

One test for identifying whether a statistic is a well-being indicator is determining where there is a consensus that if a value is high for an indicator that is a good thing or a bad thing for children. For example, there is pretty wide agreement that a high poverty rate, a high teen birth rate and a high school dropout rate are bad for children. These measures can be seen as child well-being indicators. On the other hand if one state or one country has a relatively high percentage of children age 0–4, that is not necessary a good thing or a bad thing in terms of child well-being. While making an assessment about a consensus involves some judgment, I still find it a useful approach for identifying indicators of child well-being.

The distinction between statistics and indicators is particular tricky when one is using administrative data or program participation data. For example, if a thousand children receive Supplemental Nutrition Assistance Program (SNAP) benefits (formerly known as food stamps) it is difficult to know whether that is a good thing or a bad thing for kids. It means a thousand needy children are receiving assistance (a good thing for child well-being) but it also means there are at least a thousand needy children (a bad thing for child well-being).

The same is true if the thousand children receiving SNAP benefits were put into percentage terms based on all children. If the percentage of all children receiving food stamps rises from 10 to 15 % that could mean a greater proportion of needy children are receiving assistance or it could mean there are more needy children. However, if the number of children receiving food stamps can be put into a percentage of all needy children (perhaps all of those in poverty or near poverty) it becomes much more useful as an indicator. If the percentage goes up, it signifies that more needy children are receiving the assistance they need which is generally perceived as a good thing (at least among child advocates and their allies).

Should Geographic Units be Ranked?

Among professional data analysts and statisticians ranking states, countries, or any other geographic units, in terms of child well-being is seldom used and sometimes criticized for a couple of reasons. Ranking is seen as a very limited kind of analysis, relative to more sophisticated multivariate analysis often used by scholars. Use of rankings (or more commonly a comprehensive index that is the basis of rankings) has also been criticized because it is felt child well-being measures were not broad enough or strong enough to measure differences and/or theory was not developed enough to justify combining measures into an index. Some analysts also worry that going from an index to ranking results in a "loss of information." In ranking you just know that one unit is better (or worse) than another but you don't know the distance between units.

On the other hand, ranking is a statistical technique that is easily understood by policy-makers and the public. Ranking conveys information to the public is a way that more sophisticated statistical techniques do not. It is important to recognize that providing more sophisticated statistical analysis that may be more appropriate from a scientific perspective will not be helpful if doesn't communicate information to readers, viewers or listeners of mass media.

The seductive power of rankings is described by McKenrick (2014, p. 279) as;

> Readers are inevitably drawn to the top and bottom of a league table. Favorable results are warmly received and evidenced to validate work programs and policy strategies. Adverse results occasionally lead to the methodology being questioned, but almost always lead to searching questions being asked to account for what appears to be 'poor performance.

Rankings can also be useful from an advocacy perspective because they promote competition among states to have better child outcomes than their neighboring states. Similar results in terms of public attention were achieved when countries are ranked in terms of child well-being. The state rankings provided by the KIDS COUNT report were often the lead in newspaper stories related to the KIDS COUNT release.

While rankings may seem unsophisticated to expert statisticians, scholars and researchers, the media recognizes the value of rankings and uses them often.

Does It Matter Which Geographic Units I Use?

Many data-based child advocacy reports provide a comparative perspective across units of geography. When you have a choice of geographic units, the decision about what geographic unit to use should be driven by two principals. First, people prefer to see data about the state/county/city/neighborhood where they live. Second, decisions about what level of geographic to use should be made with the policy power in mind. Using geographic units that have more policy-making authority is better than using geographic units with less policy-making authority.

There is generally a fundamental tradeoff with geographic units. Typically, there is more data available for larger units than smaller units but people generally want data for their state or local community. For example, there are many more measures of child well-being available for the U.S as a whole than for all of the states. Likewise there are more indicators available at the state level than for the county or city level. The tradeoff involves presenting a richer picture of child well-being at a higher level of geography or a more restricted view as smaller level of geography. Audiences typically like to know about the state, city or neighborhood where they live.

When deciding what geographic level to use when reporting child well-being indicators, it is important to understand and appreciate the difference between social areas and political areas. From a social science perspective, decisions about what geographic level or area to use may be driven by factors such as sample sizes, social/economic/racial homogeneity. From an advocacy point of view it is important to report on areas that have policy-making power. In the United States these are units like States, counties and cities. Geographic units like Urbanized Areas, Metropolitan, areas, regional commissions, or neighborhoods seldom have much if any policy making power.

The fact that states have a lot of responsibility for setting policies regarding children in the United States also makes state an important unit of analysis. I believe it I usually more powerful to have a few well-chosen indicators at the state and local level, than a rich set of indicators that are only available at the national level.

Again, this is involves a tradeoff between data for increasing public awareness and gaining the attention of policymakers, and data that is desired by researchers.

Identifying countries and localities within countries (States, provinces, cities) by name helps readers connect with information. In scholarly writing, specific pieces of geography such as States, or provinces, or countries, are not particularly important. If a set of countries are ranked in terms of child well-being, for example, it is the characteristics of the country are more important than the specific country from a scholarly point of view.

I don't believe there is a single right answer to this question, but I do believe that one is likely to gain more public attention by presenting a more limited set of measures for lower levels of geography. People want to know about where they live.

Should I Produce a Report Every Year?

Among scholars or scientists, once a given analysis is published, the author(s) do not feel a need to publish it again… in fact, peer-reviewed journals would never accept an update to a previously published paper.

However, in a public communication environment, one-time publications seldom move political thought. Repeating a publication "message" or topic has a much better chance of moving public opinion or political views. One saying regarding public speaking is to "Tell them what you are going to say, say it, then tell them what you said."

For example the yearly publication of the *KIDS COUNT Data Book*, the *Child Well-Being Index* reports from the Foundation for Child Development, and the Federal Interagency Forum on Child and Family Statistics *America's Children* report have been a critical element in the visibility they have achieved.

The repeated yearly publication of some reports also highlights a difference between science and communication. From a scientific perspective, it is clear that the values offered in these publications (for example child poverty, of median income) typically do not change much from one year to the next, so it is difficult to see the reason for yearly publication. However, from a communications point of view, yearly releases are important in getting public attention, elevating children's issues, and in gaining name recognition.

Regular publication also allows readers to more easily assess change over time and thus promote accountability. Use of a consistent format and consistent set of measures are also helpful in making readers more familiar with data-rich reports.

References

Child Trends. (2002). *Public Understanding of Standard Errors: A Report to the KIDS COUNT Project of the Annie E. Casey Foundation*, Child Trends, Washington, DC.

McKenrick, J. H. (2014). Geographies of child well-being; in, of and for place, In: A. Ben-Arieh, F. Casas, I. Frones & J. Korbin (Eds.) *Handbook of child well-being*, Berlin: Springer.

O'Hare, W. P. (2012). *Use of domains in indices of child wellBeing*. Presentation at International Society for Child Indicators Board Meeting, Heidelberg, Germany.

CPSIA information can be obtained at www.ICGtesting.com
Printed in the USA
LVOW01s1437030814

397297LV00005B/181/P

9 783319 078298